How to Write Like a College Student: Volume 1

By Martin Rojas

Table of Contents:

Chapter 1: How to Write ESL and Basic Skills Paragraphs 4-25

    The Classification and Division Paragraph: 9-10

    The Definition Paragraph: 11-12

    The Narration Paragraph: 13-14

    The Compare and Contrast Paragraph: 15-16

    The Illustration Paragraph: 17-18

    The Description Paragraph: 19

    The Process Analysis Paragraph: 20-21

    The Cause and Effect Paragraph: 22-23

    The Argumentative Paragraph: 24-25

Chapter 2: How to Write Five-Paragraph Essays

    The Classification and Division Essay: 33-35

    The Definition Essay: 40-42

    The Narration Essay: 45-48

    The Compare and Contrast Essay: 56-59

    The Illustration Essay: 65-67

    The Descriptive Essay: 70-72

    The Process Analysis Essay: 75-77

    The Cause and Effect Essay: 82-84

    The Argumentative Essay: 91-94

    The Timed In-Class Argumentative Essay: 104-107

    The Personal Development/Self-Reflective Essay: 108-113

IMPORTANT NOTE: PLEASE READ BEFORE PROCEEDING

This book contains paragraph and essay formats for all levels of college and high students. The book contains formats that deal with basic ESL paragraphs, five-paragraph essays, and university level critical and literary analysis essays. Each format contains step-by-step guidelines followed by sample essays. Each guideline is set up like a cooking recipe. When writing your own paragraphs and essays, follow the guidelines and samples just like you would a cooking recipe. Just follow the simple ingredients.

It is extremely important that every college student, high school student, and all other students understand that the formats in this book are **not the only way** to write these types of paragraphs and essay. The formats are a way to help all students learn how to have a thought, develop that thought, and stay on topic with that thought. These formats are designed to teach students organizational and developmental skills. Furthermore, these formats are designed to help ease the tension and anxiety of paragraph and essay writing. These formats are in no way designed to fossilize the students' creativity. After feeling more comfortable with writing, students should step outside of these formats to explore their creativity and use the formats as a backdrop for their thoughts.

When I was a student, many of my professors never gave me guidelines of what they wanted when it came to writing essays. Many of my classmates and I were always at a loss when it came to writing the essays. When I became a professor, I decided that I never wanted my students to go through what I went through. Some time ago, I started developing these formats for my students. When I saw the success rate increasing in their writing, I started sharing these formats with some of my colleagues. My colleagues began reporting to me that they were noticing rapid success rates with their students' writing. I started writing more formats, and sharing them with more and more students. Within time, these students started reporting to me that their writing has improved and their grades have increased, and those students shared my formats with other students who reported the same results.

After years of putting these formats into practice and semesters and semesters of requests, I now give the world, *How to Write Like a College Student*. This book is designed to last students from high school all the way to graduate university level writing. Students are not obligated to go through each chapter or page. For example, if you are already familiar with how to write a paragraph, then you are more then welcome to take a look at the next chapter. Furthermore, if you are already familiar with a certain type of essay in any of the chapters, feel free to look at the formats that you are not familiar with. This book is also designed as a reference book. If you are in a literature course and know how to write about a character but not the setting, then feel free to look up the format that you need. Happy writing!

Chapter 1: How to Write ESL and Basic Skills Paragraphs

What is an ESL Paragraph?

ESL stands for English as a Second Language. Many colleges in the United States have students whose second language is English. The English language is perhaps one of the most difficult languages to learn and master because it has so many rules; moreover, there are so many exceptions to those rules. This can be challenging too many ESL students. Therefore, many colleges require that these students complete an ESL program. The ESL program helps build English reading, writing, and speaking skills. Most ESL courses will start off with grammar lessons and paragraph writing. The ESL paragraph is a basic type of paragraph, which differs from other types of paragraphs.

The ESL paragraph is a very basic form of writing. It consists of all the elements that a paragraph needs for full development and organization. This type of paragraph should be anywhere from 5 to 10 sentences long. It can be a little longer, but it should not be overly lengthy. 15 sentences maximum is more than enough for the ESL paragraph. This type of paragraph should always use reasons and examples.

The most distinguishing factors of the ESL paragraph are that they are basic, and they are short and to the point. The ESL paragraph also does not contain the most sophisticated writing style, such as extremely high-level vocabulary. This type of paragraph also rarely demonstrates the highest level of sentence variety. For the most part, these sentences will only demonstrate the basic form of simple sentences, compound sentences, complex sentences, and compound complex sentences.

This type of paragraph will provide a very clear and specific topic sentence. There should also be several supporting detail sentences that fully elaborate and explain the topic sentence. Students should also end with a nice closing sentence that reinforces the topic sentence and the main points of the overall paragraph. The topic sentence should specifically tell what the entire paragraph will be about.

For ESL students, the topic sentence is not going to be the most sophisticated. In other words, the topic sentence will be short and to the point. For example, if you are going to write about why the beach is your favorite place, then your topic sentence will read something along the lines of: "My favorite place is the beach because it is peaceful, beautiful, and warm."

The body sentences will discuss and elaborate on the topic sentence. In this case, the body sentences will explore the three main reasons why you like the beach. The body sentences should explain each reason that you like the beach and provide specific and personal examples that will highlight your explanations. The closing sentence will simply seal off the entire paragraph.

Different Types of ESL Paragraphs

ESL stands for English as a second language. Most colleges will offer various ESL programs and classes. These classes are designed to teach ESL students how to become more sufficient writers and readers of the English language. These types of classes will teach ESL students about the rules of grammar, mechanics, paragraph writing, and essay writing. One of the main courses that ESL students will face deals with basic paragraph writing. Students will face numerous genres of paragraphs in this type of a course. This article will list and define the different types of ESL paragraphs.

The Classification and Division Paragraph: This type of paragraph will ask students to pick one element or object that they know well and divide it into three categories. For example, students can pick three items in their bedroom and divide into three categories, such as clothes, furniture, and toys. Students will explore these three categories in their paragraph.

The Definition Paragraph: This type of paragraph will ask students to pick one word or object and define what it means to them. For the most part, students will take this word or object and provide three key words or phrases that define what it means to them. For example, students could pick three key words to define the word "home."

The Narration Paragraph: This type of paragraph will ask students to write a first person story. For the most part, this type of paragraph will ask students to write about one life changing moment in their life and provide an adjective that describes that moment.

The Compare and Contrast Paragraph: This type of paragraph will ask students to take two to three objects and write about how they are similar and how they are different. For example, students can write about two or three holidays in their home countries and compare and contrast them with how the United States celebrates these holidays.

The Illustration Paragraph: This type of paragraph asks student to provide reasons and examples. Students are to pick a subject and tell why they like it or dislike it. Students will need to pick at least three key words or phrases to tell why they like or dislike the topic that they are writing about. Students can write about a person, place, or thing.

The Description Paragraph: This type of paragraph will ask students to describe a person, place, or thing. Students will pick three key words or phrases that will allow them to describe the noun. The three words or phrases will be explored in the paragraph.

The Process Analysis Paragraph: This type of paragraph will ask student to write step-by-step instruction on how to do a particular thing. Students will write about something that they know how to do well.

The Cause and Effect Paragraph: This type of paragraph will ask students to pick one element or object and list either three causes or three effects of that object or element. For example, students may list and explore the three effects of smoking.

The Argumentative Paragraph: This type of paragraph will ask students to take a stand for or against a controversial issue. Students will pick three words or phrases that will defend their argument. If students are for an issue, they need to explore three words or phrases that tell why. If students are against an issue, they need to list and explore three words or phrases that tell why.

How to Prewrite an ESL Paragraph

Prewriting allows all writers, especially college students, to properly plan out their essays and paragraphs. Prewriting will help ensure that all writers fully develop their thoughts and stay on topic with those thoughts. Furthermore, when students and other writers take the time to prewrite, it can help prevent writer's block. Perhaps ESL students will gain the most benefit with their writing if they take the proper time to prewrite since English can be a challenge for those who have it as their second language. This section will teach college ESL students how to prewrite the basic paragraph.

Step 1: There are a number or prewriting activities that ESL students can do to prewrite their work. These activities include clustering, free writing, listing, and outlining. Outlining is perhaps one of the most effective prewriting techniques for ESL students. However, each student will notice that prewriting will only work if he or she uses the technique that is most comfortable for him or her.

Step 2: Whether you decide to cluster or list or use another technique, it is important to take time to fully understand the topic that your instructor is asking you to write about. Most ESL students will benefit from viewing several examples of fully developed paragraphs that previous students have written. When reading other sample paragraphs, take time to read the examples several times. Be sure to absorb the format, the sentence structure, the development, and the content. When you take time to view several examples, it will give you an idea of how to approach your paragraph.

Step 3: Take time to jot down a few ideas regarding your topic. For example, if your assignment is to write a paragraph that discusses three unique cultural traditions regarding Christmas in your country, then take time to think about three things that your country does for Christmas that people in the United States do not do. Write these ideas down on paper. Your ideas do not have to be complete sentences, as you are only prewriting.

Step 4: Be sure to narrow down your ideas to three main things that you would really like to explore. Outline each idea with a brief explanation. After outlining your explanations, it is a good idea to outline some specific example that will highlight your explanations. Be sure that you put your examples directly under your explanations. It is also a good idea to begin your prewriting with a topic sentence that you will begin your actual paragraph with. If your prewriting contains the topic sentence and an outline of your explanations and examples of three things that you will discuss, then you will have an easy time constructing your final paragraph draft.

How to Write a Well-Developed and Organized Classification ESL Paragraph

The classification paragraph asks students to examine one element or object and divide that one element/object into three categories. This type of paragraph allows students to become more analytical when it comes to dividing and classifying things. Moreover, this type of paragraph allows the writer to give the reader a new way to look at things; it gives the reader a different way to categorize his/her own similar objects. This section will teach ESL and basic skills students how to write a classification paragraph.

Note: Be sure that you follow the lower case letters in the format and sample paragraphs as you would a cooking recipe. The lower case letters are the ingredients.

Format/Recipe of a Classification Paragraph:

a) Write one topic sentence that mentions the element you will discuss and include three key words or phrases that tell how you divide this one element.

b) In about one to two sentences explain your first key word. Tell why you divide this element into that one category.

c) Give a two-sentence example that illustrates your explanation.

d) Using a transition phrase, write one to two sentences that explain your second category.

e) Give another two-sentence example that illustrates your explanation.

f) Starting with another transition phrase, write one to sentences that explain your third category from your topic sentence.

g) Give another specific example of your third category.

h) Write one closing sentence.

Sample Classification Paragraph:

(**a**) I classify my shirts into three categories, which are street shirts, work shirts, and formal shirts. (**b**) I first categorize my shirts by street shirts because I have many, and I like to spend a lot of time outdoors with my friends. For example, most of my street shirts are white t-shirts. The other day I went to the lake with my friends, and my street shirt was perfect to wear. (**c**) Second, I classify my shirts by work shirts because I work five days a week, and like to wear a different shirt for every day of the week in case one gets dirty. (**d**) For instance, one Monday I wore my white work shirt, but I spilled coffee on it in the middle of the day. Well, on Tuesday I was able to wear my green work shirt. (**e**) Finally, I have a formal shirt category, which is limited because I do not attend many formal events. (**f**) To illustrate, I only attended two formal events last year, which were one wedding and one graduation. The small category of formal shirts allowed me to be prepared for these two events. **(h)** These are the three categories that I classify my shirts into.

How to Write a Definition ESL Paragraph

The definition paragraph asks students to take one element or object that they know well and define it. This type of paragraph asks students to tell what that one element/object means to them. Moreover, students are asked to provide three key words or phrases that will allow them to define that one element/object. This section will teach ESL and basic skills students how to write a full developed and well-organized definition paragraph.

Note: Be sure that you follow the lower case letters in the format and sample paragraphs as you would a cooking recipe. The lower case letters are the ingredients.

Format/Recipe for a Definition Paragraph:

a) Write one topic sentence that mentions the element or object that you will define. Your topic sentence should also include three key words or phrases that define your element/object.

b) Write one to two sentences that explain your first defining word from your topic sentence.

c) Provide a two-sentence specific example that will illustrate your explanation.

d) Using a transitional phrase, write one to two sentences that explain your second defining word.

e) Give another two-sentence example that shows your explanation.

f) Explain your final defining word in about one to two sentences.

g) Provide another specific example to illustrate your third defining word.

h) Write one closing sentence to seal off your paragraph.

Sample of a Definition Paragraph:

(a) For me, family can be defined as trustworthy, loving, and non-judgmental. **(b)** I first define family as trustworthy because people should always be able to tell family anything, and family should respect any secrets. **(c)** For example, my cousins, aunt, and mom have kept one of my biggest secrets to themselves and have never told anyone outside the family. To me, that is trustworthy. **(d)** I also define family as loving because they should always be there for me and encourage me to get through life's little struggles. **(e)** To illustrate, I failed a big exam once, which meant I only had one more chance to pass my class. Well, when I wanted to give up, my family showed me much love through their support. **(f)** I finally define family as non-judgmental because I never feel uncomfortable to share words or actions with my family; they should accept me no matter what. **(g)** For instance, I have a friend who is gay. When he told his family that he was gay, they rejected him. A real family would have accepted him no matter what and not judge him. **(h)** These are the three ways that I define family.

How to Write a Well-Developed and Organized Narration ESL Paragraph

The narration paragraph asks students to relive one life-changing moment in their lives and write about it. This type of writing asks students to tell about the situation that changed their lives, give an adjective that describes that situation, tell what happened during that situation, tell about their thoughts and emotions during that situation, tell what they learned from that situation or how it changed them, and leave something behind for their readers, such as advice or a moral. Furthermore, the narration paragraph asks students to describe their thoughts about that situation to ultimately make the reader feel what the writer felt at that time. This type of paragraph asks students to face the past and have a responsible acceptance of that past. Their subject matter can be about any type of emotion, such as happiness, sadness, anxiety, humor, fear, etc. This section will provide step-by-step instructions and a sample paragraph that will teach students how to write a fully developed and well-organized narration paragraph.

Note: The following format and sample paragraph contain lower cases letters, which help students when they write their own narrations. Just think of the lower case letters as cooking ingredients; follow the simple recipe.

Format/Recipe for a Narration Paragraph:

a) Write one topic sentence that states the incident you will write about and include an adjective that describes the situation.

b) Provide one sentence that states the point or moral of your story. Your point/moral should be the lesson that you learned or how the situation changed you.

c) In one to two sentences, tell how your story began.

d) Write one to two sentences that describe your thoughts and emotions. Tell what went through your mind. Make comparisons to other objects and your senses.

e) Using a transitional phrase, tell about the second major event in the incident that you are writing about. Tell what happened next in about one to two sentences.

f) In about one to two sentences, describe your thoughts and emotions. Again make comparisons to things.

g) Tell about the third and final event in your situation. Again, this should be done in about one to two sentences.

h) Describe your thoughts and emotions once again.

i) End your paragraph with resolution and advice for your reader.

Sample Narration Paragraph:

(a) The saddest day of my life was when my best friend of nine years died. (b) From this situation, I learned that life can end at any time and people should always cherish their loved ones. (c) My best friend got accepted into medical school across seas. A few weeks after being there, someone stabbed him. (d) When I got the news, my mind froze. I lost all control of my senses; I felt like someone took me out of a hot tub and threw me in zero degree water. (e) After receiving the news, my friend's family had his body shipped back to the states. We all went to his funeral. (f) At the funeral, I was catatonic; everyone was catatonic. My thoughts were a jumbled pile of broken bottles waiting to be recycled, and the sound of bottles breaking kept ringing in my ears. (g) Several months passed, and I could not bring myself to go and visit his family; I do not know why, scared I guess. However, I finally made it to his family, and they seemed to be coping with things better than me. (h) From seeing them, I knew things would be okay. My friend's spirit was with us, and I instantly felt a relief of the pressure that was building up in my head, body, and soul. (i) Everyone loses people they love, but when that happens, just know that they are always watching over us, and everything always heals in time; the pain heals slowly but surely.

How to Write a Fully Developed and Well-Organized Compare and Contrast ESL Paragraph

The compare and contrast paragraph asks students to pick two elements or objects from their life and write about the similarities and differences. Students are to examine the similarities and/or differences. This type of paragraph requires that students write about these similarities and differences in a nice and controlled way, in which they stay 100% on topic. This section will provide clear and focused step-by-step instructions on how to write a basic compare and contrast paragraph. A sample paragraph will also be provided.

Note: Please follow the format and sample paragraph as you would a cooking recipe. All of the ingredients are provided. Also, note that the number of sentences that I say to write is only a guideline for organization and development. You are free to write a little less or a little more.

Format/Recipe for a Compare and Contrast Paragraph:

a). Write one topic sentence that provides the element/objects that you will be comparing and contrasting. Make sure you mention how they are the same but different.

b). In about one sentence, mention the first similarity, but fully explain the difference within that similarity.

c). Provide a two-sentence example of the first difference.

d). With one transitional phrase, explain your second similarity and the difference within that similarity.

e). In about two sentences, give another illustrative example of the second difference.

f). Explain your third similarity and difference in about one sentence, and be sure to start with a transitional phrase.

g). Give one last example of your third difference in about two sentences.

h). Write one closing sentence to seal off your paragraph.

Sample Compare and Contrast Paragraph:

(a) Although my mom and dad's apartment complexes have the same amount of units, have a lot of residences, and have two pools, one complex is older, has a lower class of people, and one set of pools is dirty. **(b)** While my mom and dad both live in large apartment complexes, my dad's is extremely old, while my mom's is new. **(c)** For example, there are broken stairs and peeling paint all throughout my dad's complex. On the other hand, my mom has brand new paint and brand new stairs. **(d)** Furthermore, my dad's complex has some of the worst tenants, while my mom has upper class people living at her complex. **(e)** To illustrate, the cops are at my dad's complex about three to four nights a week arresting tenants for drugs and violence. The tenants at my mom's place consist of doctors and lawyers. **(f)** Finally, the two pools at my father's place are disgusting, while my mom's are perfectly kept up. **(g)** For instance, the pool water at my dad's is always green and the walls are black with mold. My mom's pools are crystal clear, and the pool guy cleans it every day. **(h)** As you can see, my parents' apartment complexes share similarity in size, the amount of tenants, and two pools; however, there are distinct differences within those similarities.

How to Write a Fully Developed ESL Illustration Paragraph

Many college ESL (English Second Language) and basic skills English courses will have their students write one illustration paragraph. The purpose of this kind of writing and other paragraph writing is to teach students how develop and organize their thoughts. The illustration paragraph requires that students discuss whether or not they like or dislike a particular person, place, or thing and give reasons and examples that explain and show why. The purpose of this section is to show ESL and basic skills students a way to stay fully developed and organized with their thoughts. This section will provide step-by-step information and two examples of how to write a fully developed and well-organized illustration paragraph.

Note: The following format and sample paragraphs work like a cooking recipe. The lower case letters are the ingredients that belong in your own illustration paragraph.

Recipe/Format for an Illustration Paragraph:

a). Write one topic sentence that discusses the element or object that you will be writing about. In this sentence, you should tell if you like or dislike your topic and have three reasons why.

b). In one sentence, explain your first reason. Your explanation should explain why you feel the way you do.

c). Give one specific example that will illustrate your first explanation.

d). Be sure to explain your second reason in one sentence and start with a transitional phrase.

e). Provide a clear and specific example that supports your second explanation. Your example should be no more than two sentences.

f). Using another transitional phrase, write one sentence that explains your third reason.

g). Write about two sentences that give an illustrative example of your third reason.

h). Seal off your entire paragraph with one closing sentence.

Sample of an Illustration Paragraph:

(a) I love my English class because my professor is funny, my classmates are friendly, and the reading is fun. **(b)** First of all, my English professor is funny because he is always impersonating famous people and characters from movies. **(c)** To illustrate, the other day he imitated The Joker from the movie, *The Dark Knight*. My professor sounded just like Heath Ledger who played The Joker. **(d)** Another reason why I like my English class is because my classmates are very friendly which makes class more entertaining. **(e)** For example, everyday my classmates and I visit before class and after class. We also form great groups during group work in which we help each other out and make each other laugh. **(f)** Finally, I love my English class because the reading is really fun which gives me motivation to read. **(g)** For instance, I am not a reader; however, we had to read Sherman Alexie's, *The Absolutely True Diary of a Part-Time Indian*. This book was so funny and captivating that I could not put it down. **(h)** For all these reasons, I love my English class.

Sample 2:

(a) I love walking in the park because it is peaceful, scenic, and social. **(b)** The park is peaceful to walk in because there are so many peaceful sounds. **(c)** For example, every time I walk in the park, I hear birds chirping and people laughing; these are both peaceful sounds. **(d)** Second, I love the scenery at the park because it offers an escape from the city life. **(e)** For instance, the park is full of green trees that create a forest atmosphere, and there is a huge lake that looks natural and calm. **(f)** Finally, I love walking in the park because it is social, and that takes away any lonely feeling. **(g)** Every time I walk in the park, I see people talking to each other and having a great time. People are always talking to me, and I am always talking to them. **(h)** These are the three reasons why I love walking at the park.

Notice how the above sample paragraphs follows the format/recipe.

How to Write a Fully Developed and Well-Organized Descriptive ESL Paragraph

The descriptive paragraph is designed to teach ESL students how to describe one person, place or thing. This type of paragraph will usually require that the students pick one noun and add three adjectives that will describe it. These adjectives will be explored in the paragraph. This section will teach ESL students how to write a descriptive paragraph. There will also be a sample paragraph that follows the recipe.

Format/Recipe for a Descriptive Paragraph:

a). Write one sentence that mentions the person, place, or thing that you will describe. Your sentence should also include three adjectives that will describe the noun.

b). In about one sentence, explain what you mean by the first adjective from your topic sentence.

c). Give a one to two sentence example that supports your first explanation.

d). Using a transitional phrase, explain your second adjective from your topic sentence.

e). Write another specific and clear two to three sentence example that illustrates your second explanation.

f). Starting with another transitional phrase, explain your third adjective from your topic sentence.

g). Write another clear and specific example of the third adjective.

h). End your paragraph with a closing sentence.

Sample Definition Paragraph:

(a) My best friend John has three unique characteristics; he is extremely hyper, outspoken, and rude. **(b)** To begin with, John is extremely hyper active. He never sits still or stops talking. **(c)** For example, the other day a group of us were out of town all day. By the end of the day, we were all tired, but John still wanted to go out and party. **(d)** John is also very outspoken. He will have the most inappropriate conversations in public or say things that he should not say in public. **(e)** To illustrate, two weeks ago I was at a store with John. While we were in line, he was telling me a vulgar story while others were around; everyone kept starring. **(f)** Finally, John is rude and will do what he wants no matter who is around. **(g)** One day a group of people was waiting for a store to open. Well, John cut in front of everybody and acted as if it was nothing. **(h)** These are three things that best describe John.

How to Write a Well-Developed Process Analysis ESL Paragraph

The process analysis works like a "how to" guideline. For this assignment, students will be asked to pick one thing that they know how to do well and provide step-by-step instructions for their reader to follow. Students can write about anything that they want for this assignment, but they need to make sure that they know a lot about it. For example, students could write out cooking instructions, home repair, car repair, health care instructions, etc. This section will teach students how to write a process analysis paragraph.

Note: This article will contain a step-by-step format to follow and a sample process analysis paragraph. The format and sample will contain lower case letters, which are designed for students to use as a checklist for their own writing. The lower case letters work like a cooking recipe; just follow the simple ingredients.

Format/Recipe for the Process Analysis Paragraph:

a) Write one sentence that will mention the topic that you will discuss, and mention how many steps there are to follow. Your paragraph should contain no more than three to four steps.

b) In one sentence, mention your first step.

c) Explain your first step in about two sentences. Be sure to be clear in your explanation.

d) Using a transitional phrase, state your second step.

e) In about two sentences, explain your second step nice and clearly.

f) Starting with another transitional phrase, tell your third step in one sentence.

g) Clearly explain your third step in about two sentences.

h) Write one closing sentence that will seal off your entire paragraph.

Sample Process Analysis Paragraph:

(a) There are three basic steps to follow when properly cleaning your teeth. **(b)** The first step is to rinse your mouth out with warm water. **(c)** Rinsing your mouth out with warm water will loosen any food stuck between your teeth. Rinsing your mouth also loosens up any bacteria or tartar built up from the day. **(d)** The second step is to floss all areas of your teeth. **(e)** Flossing your teeth will get all the food and bacteria built up out from between your teeth, which can prevent future infection and cavities. **(f)** The final step is to thoroughly brush your teeth with toothpaste and rinse with mouthwash. **(g)** Brushing your teeth and rinsing with mouthwash removes all excess food and bacteria buildup. It also keeps your teeth white and your breath fresh. **(h)** These are the three basic steps to follow when it comes to properly cleaning your teeth.

How to Write a Well-Developed Cause and Effect ESL Paragraph

The cause and effect paragraph asks students to examine one element and describe how one cause can create three effects for that element. For example, a student could write about three negative effects that arise from smoking. Another option that students have is to write about the three causes of something derived from one effect. This section will teach ESL and basic skills students how to write a fully developed and well-organized cause and effect paragraph.

Note: The lower case letters contain a step-by-step format that students should follow in order to construct an organized cause and effect paragraph. Moreover, the sample paragraph, which appears below the format, will also contain the lower case letters, so that students can easily follow along. Be sure to think of the format and sample paragraph as a cooking recipe.

Recipe/Format for the Cause and Effect Paragraph:

   a) Write one sentence that mentions one cause and three effects of that cause.

   b) Write one to two sentences that explain the first effect.

   c) In about two sentences, provide an example of that effect.

   d) Using a transition phrase, write one sentence that explains the second effect.

   e) Give another two-sentence example of the second effect. Make sure your example is specific.

   f) Using another transitional phrase, explain the third effect.

   g) In another two sentences, give a specific example of the third effect.

   h) Write one closing sentence that will seal off your entire paragraph.

Sample Cause and Effect Paragraph:

(a) There are many things that cause a person to drink alcohol; however, there are three negative effects that derive from dinking too many alcoholic beverages, which are liver damage, brain damage, and relationship damage. **(b)** First of all, alcohol causes liver damage because the human body cannot constantly expel all the toxins that alcohol contains. **(c)** For example, my uncle was an excessive drinker, and he died from liver failure. The doctors said his liver gave out from all the alcohol. **(d)** Another effect of alcohol is brain damage. Alcohol kills brains cells, which decreases our memory. **(e)** For instance, my friend's father has been an alcoholic for over 20 years. Well, his father always forgets people's names and conversations that he just had. **(f)** Finally, alcohol destroys relationships because it can emotionally and sometimes physically hurt the people who are around the drinker. (**g**) To illustrate, I watched a movie about a man who drink so much that he would come home and beat his wife and kids. (**h**) These are the three negative effects of drinking alcohol.

How to Write a Fully Developed and Well-Organized ESL Argumentative

The argumentative paragraph asks students to take a stand and defend that stand. This section will discuss a step-by-step format to follow for writing one argumentative paragraph; furthermore, one example of an argumentative paragraph will be provided.

Note: Be sure that you follow the lower case letters in the format and sample paragraphs as you would a cooking recipe. The lower case letters are the ingredients.

Format/Recipe for an Argumentative Paragraph:

a). Write one topic sentence. Your topic sentence should state your side of the argument and have three reasons why you feel the way you do.

b). Explain your first reason in about one sentence.

c). Provide a one to two sentence example that supports your first explanation.

d). Using a transitional phrase, explain your second reason. Your explanation should be no longer than one sentence.

e). Write two to three sentences of a clear and specific example that supports your second explanation.

f). Starting with another transitional phrase and in one sentence, explain your third reason.

g). Give another two to three sentence example that supports your third explanation.

h). Write one closing sentence to end your paragraph.

Sample of an Argumentative Paragraph:

(**a**) I believe that people who are twelve years old and up should receive sex education classes because this age group reaches puberty, it could prevent teen pregnancies, and it could prevent STD's. (**b**) I first believe that sex education should be taught at the age of twelve and older because puberty makes teens curious and confused. (**c**) For example, when my cousin reached twelve, he was confused and did not understand his own body, so he had sex and regretted it. (**d**) I also believe that sex education could prevent pregnancies because of the stories that other teen mothers would share. (**e**) For instance, my sister took sex education at the age of 13. She was curious about sex; however, after hearing the stories of the suffering that other teen mothers went through, my sister decided to wait. (**f**) Finally, I believe that sex education could prevent STD's for teenagers because it would bring awareness to them. (**g**) To illustrate, my neighbor's son was unaware of safe sex, and at the age of fourteen, he contracted an STD. (**h**) For all these reasons, I believe that sex education should be taught to people who are twelve years old and up.

Notice how the above sample paragraph 100% follows the format/recipe.

Chapter 2: How to Write Five-Paragraph Essays

IMPORTANT NOTE: PLEASE READ BEFORE PROCEEDING

The following chapter contains essay formats and samples of almost every type of five-paragraph essay. Each type of essay will first begin with the recipes/formats and samples of those recipes/formats. These recipes/formats and samples contain information on how to write all five paragraphs (e.g. introduction, three body paragraphs, and conclusion). Remember to follow every format as you would a cooking recipe. Just follow the simple ingredients. After each individual format, there will be supplementary information to help elaborate on the formats.

The supplementary information is designed to help clarify any uncertainties that students may feel on certain aspects of the full-length formats. Each essay format will contain supplemental information. For example, one type of essay may contain supplementary information on how to write the conclusion and introduction. On the other hand, another type of essay may contain supplementary information on how to write the thesis statement, introduction, and body paragraphs. The students' main information and lessons will come from the full-length formats. Before the formats, enjoy some information that discusses the various five-paragraph essays.

What is a Five-Paragraph Essay?

Most college students will write a number of five-paragraph essays in their preparatory English courses. The purpose of the five-paragraph essay is to teach students how to organize and develop their thoughts. Moreover, the five-paragraph essay is designed to prepare students for more advanced essay writing. This type of essay will help students feel more comfortable when it comes to essay writing. This section will describe, in detail, what the five-paragraph essay is and provide descriptions of various types.

The five-paragraph essay consists of an introduction, three body paragraphs, and a conclusion. Each paragraph needs to be fully developed and well organized. Furthermore, each paragraph needs to stay on topic and be treated with equal length. For the most part, each paragraph in the five-paragraph essay will consist of seven to fifteen sentences. Each paragraph can be longer or shorter, but seven to fifteen sentences are standard.

The introduction will provide information about the topic that is being written about, and includes a thesis statement, which will usually be one sentence that provides three key words or phrases that will be discussed in each body paragraph. There will be three body paragraphs that need to fully support the thesis statement. Each body paragraph will provide an explanation of each key word or phrase from the thesis statement, and there will be a clear and specific example in each body paragraph. The example will support each explanation. Finally, there needs to be a closing sentence in each body paragraph.

All five-paragraph essays will end with a conclusion. The conclusion will basically summarize all of the main points from the entire essay. The conclusion should re-mention the thesis statement, and there should be a brief recap of all the specific examples from the body paragraphs. Every conclusion should end with a couple of final thoughts about the overall topic.

Various Types of Five-Body Paragraph Essays

The Five-Classification Essay: This type of essay asks students to pick one element and divide that element into sub-categories. This type essay asks students to divide that element into three categories. For example, a student can write about three categories that he/she divides his/her DVD collection into.

The Five-Paragraph Definition Essay: This type of essay asks students to pick one element or object and define what that element or object means to them. This type of essay asks students to pick three defining words or short phrases that give meaning to the topic that they are writing about. For this kind of an essay, the writer does not need to rely on the dictionary; the writer defines the object or element and shares what it means to him or her.

The Five-Paragraph Narration Essay: This type of essay asks students to examine one incident or fragment from their past and write about that past in the first person. In this type of essay, students will tell the story of that past and describe all their emotions and thoughts about that past. Usually, the narration essay will offer the reader a lesson or moral that the actual writer learned from that past.

The Five-Paragraph Compare and Contrast Essay: This type of essay asks students to examine two elements. The student will write how those two elements are similar but different at the same time. In other words, this type of essay asks student to pick three similarities between two objects, write about those similarities, and write about the three differences within those similarities.

The Five-Paragraph Illustration Essay: This type of essay asks students to provide explanations and very clear examples for the topic that they are writing about. To illustrate means to explain and show examples. Students should not confuse this type of essay with a descriptive essay. The illustration essay does not require description, only facts and examples.

The Five-Paragraph Description Essay: This type of essay asks students to clearly describe a place, person, or thing. This type of essay will allow students to paint a picture by using words. Furthermore, this type of essay asks students to make comparisons to things, so their readers can get an image in their minds while reading. For example, students could compare whatever they are writing about to the five senses. Moreover, this type of essay asks students to use a lot of metaphors and similes for better description.

The Five-Paragraph Process Analysis Essay: This type of essay asks students to write out step-by-step instructions or guidelines for a particular task. This type of essay works like a "how to" article. Furthermore, this type of essay asks students to write about something they are highly knowledgeable about and teach their readers how to do something. Students are free to write about anything they want, but it must be in the "how to" format.

The Five-Paragraph Cause and Effect Essay: This type of essay asks students to think of the actual cause of something, and then write about the three effects that develop from that cause. This type of essay allows the writer to warn his/her readers about the effects of certain things, such as too much sun or too much unhealthy food.

The Five-Paragraph Argumentative Essay: This type of essay asks students to take a stand on a particular issue. For this type of essay, students are required to pick one side; they are either for or against a particular issue. Students cannot be in between an issue; they have to pick one side only. For this type of essay, students will pick three clear reasons why they are either for or against a particular issue. Furthermore, this type of essay asks students to fully explain each of their reasons and use very clear and specific examples to support their reasons.

What Is a Thesis Statement?

A thesis statement is perhaps one of the most important components of an essay. There are so many college students who go through college not fully understanding what a thesis statement is. Many college students will simply learn that a thesis statement is what the entire essay will be about. Well, the fact that a thesis statement is what the essay is about is only part of the full meaning. This article will describe in detail what a thesis statement is.

A thesis statement will state the entire purpose of the essay. It is the statement that will show the reader what the writer will argue and prove. Depending on the type of essay, the thesis statement is usually no more than three sentences long. It can be longer, and it can be shorter, but generally college students will write a thesis statement that is roughly around three sentences. For the five-paragraph essay, most thesis statements will be one sentence. Although a thesis statement is short, it needs to be extremely detailed and thorough. It needs to tell exactly what the essay will provide and how the information will be backed up.

There will not be any generalities in the thesis statement; it will be direct and to the point. For the most part, the thesis statement will appear at the end of the introduction paragraph. A thesis statement does not have to appear as the last sentence in the introduction; however, most college students will have it appear at the end of their introduction. They are either used to writing the thesis at the end of the introduction, or their professor asks them to. One thing to keep in mind is that many scholarly articles will not have a thesis statement at the end of the introduction. Some may appear in the middle of the second paragraph or in other places

When writing a thesis statement, it is important to think about your purpose, think about your argument, think about what you want to teach your reader, and think about how you will prove and defend your point and argument. If you can answer all of the above, then you will be able to articulate a solid and coherent thesis statement. For the most part, the thesis statement will not leave anything open; it will state exactly what you will cover and prove. Again, it needs to be short, but it needs to be fully detailed. Most thesis statements will discuss your main points in the order that you will discuss them in your essay body paragraphs.

The Importance of Prewriting

Prewriting can be done in a number of ways; it can be outlining, clustering, free writing, listing, diagraming, etc. Prewriting is one of the most important parts of submitting a successful piece of writing. This is true for all writers, especially college students. There are so many college students who do not take the proper amount of time to prewrite their essays. As a result, many students become disappointed when their grades are not what they are hoping for. Whether many students are lazy or just do not know how to prewrite, it is always important to prewrite your work. This article will discuss the importance of essay prewriting.

When students take time to prewrite their essays, it helps them to form more coherent and well-developed thoughts. When you are writing an essay, many professors will look for thought fluency and development of paragraphs. The prewriting will allow students to take time and think about what they want to write and say about the topic. It also allows them to plan out how many sentences each paragraph should approximately be.

There are many students who have trouble starting their essays and developing a fully articulated thesis statement. Well, any type of prewriting exercise will help students brainstorm their introductions and thesis statement. The thesis statement is perhaps one of the most important parts of the essay because it tells the reader exactly what the essay will explain, show, and prove. Therefore, it is important to take time and think about the thesis statement. Prewriting will allow college students time to do so.

Another important aspect of prewriting is the notion of organization. When students prewrite, it gives them the opportunity to organize all of their paragraphs. Furthermore, it gives them the opportunity to decide how they want to lay out their ideas and the order in which their ideas should appear. College professors always look for fully organized essays. Prewriting will help students determine what belongs in their paragraphs and what does not.

There are many college students who suffer from writer's block. Well, when students take the time to prewrite, it can actually help break the block because prewriting allows the thoughts to flow out freely. When students take the time to prewrite, many will notice that they do not struggle with their official essays as much. Therefore, it is important to prewrite all essays and important to find the type of prewriting that is most suitable for each individual student.

Prewriting can also prevent errors. When students do prewriting, it can prevent grammatical and mechanical errors in their final drafts. It is important that all essay are free of these errors, and prewriting will help with that. When students do not prewrite and just attempt to start writing the essay, they only focus on trying to stay organized and on topic; therefore, they do not stay fully focused on their grammar and mechanics. Therefore, when students prewrite, they have an idea of what to write for their essays, which means they can focus on grammar and mechanics much more.

The Five-Paragraph Classification Essay

How to Write a Five-Paragraph Classification Essay

Many college freshmen will be asked to write a five-paragraph classification essay in their preparatory English courses. The classification essay, also known as the division essay, asks students to pick one element or object and divide it into three categories. For example, a student could write about his/her DVD collection and discuss how that collection is divided into three categories. Just as all other five-paragraph essays, this essay will also have an introduction, three body paragraphs, and a conclusion. The three categories will be discussed in the three body paragraphs. This section will teach students how to write a fully developed and well-organized five-paragraph classification essay.

Note: The following formats for each paragraph work like a cooking recipe; be sure to follow the simple ingredients. Furthermore, for each sample paragraph, I provide lower case letters to illustrate the paragraph recipe/formats.

I. Recipe/Format for an Introduction:

a). Start with about two to three sentences of general statements about the object or element that you will be classifying.

b). Write about two sentences that discuss some possible ways other people would classify the element/object that you are writing about.

c). In one sentence, state your thesis. Your thesis statement will mention the element/object that you are classifying, and it will mention the three categories that you are dividing this element into.

Sample of an Introduction:

(a) There are many people who have a big collection of shoes. Many people use their various shoes for various reasons. Moreover, there are many people who collect shoes for the sake of collecting them. (b) There are some people who like to classify their shoes by brand names. Moreover, there are people who like to divide their shoes by color. (c) I like to classify my shoe collection into three categories, which are work shoes, dress shoes, and exercise shoes.

II. Recipe/Format for the 1st Body Paragraph:

(a). In about two to three sentences, explain your first category from your thesis statement. Tell why you like to classify/divide your element or object into this category.

(b). Write three to four sentences that provide a specific and clear example that illustrates your explanation.

(c). Seal off your paragraph with one closing sentence.

Sample of the 1st Body Paragraph:

(a) My first category is my work shoes. I own more of these shoes than any other kind. My work shoes are mostly dress shoes; they actually resemble work boots and/or hiking shoes. I like to have a work shoe category because I love to have a different pairs of shoes for every day of the week, especially if one pair gets dirty. **(b)** For example, on Monday, I wore my black work shoes, and they are really comfortable. However, they got dirty because I stepped in some mud, and I did not have time to clean them. Therefore, on Tuesday, I was able to wear my brown work shoes. **(c)** It is convenient having a category for my work shoes.

III. Recipe/Format for the 2nd Body Paragraph:

a). Using a transitional phrase, write two to three sentences that explain the reason for your second category from your thesis statement.

b). In about three to four sentences provide another illustrative example of your second category.

c) Write one closing sentence to seal off the paragraph.

Sample of the 2nd Body Paragraph:

(a) I also have a category of dress shoes because I go to a lot of formal functions. I have a large family and many friends, and there is always a wedding to attend. Therefore, I like to have a variety of dress shoes to choose from, so that I do not have to go shopping for a pair the night before a formal function. **(b)** For instance, the other night, I received a call that my cousin was getting married the next day. My cousin wanted me to be at the wedding. Well, I was not stressed because I already had a collection of dress shoes to choose from. **(c)** If I did not have this category of shoes, then I probably would have been stressed having to shop for shoes the day before my cousin's wedding.

IV. Recipe/Format for the 3rd Body Paragraph:

a). Explain your third category form your thesis in about two to three sentences, and do start with a transitional phrase.

b). Write a three to four sentence specific example that will support your third explanation.

(c). End your paragraph with one closing sentence.

Sample of the 3rd Body Paragraph:

(**a**) My final category is my exercise shoes. I love to walk and run; therefore, it is important to have a decent pair of exercise shoes to prevent injury. My exercise shoes mostly consist of Nike and New Balance brand names, and I like to use a different brand for different exercises. (**b**) For example, when I walk, I find that my Nike shoes are much more comfortable. One day I tried walking in my New Balance shoes, but my back felt uncomfortable, so I use Nike to walk. On the other hand, I love my New Balance shoes when I run. I found Nike does not work for me when I run. (**c**) I love my category of exercise shoes.

Recipe/Format for a Conclusion:

a). In about two sentences re-state your thesis statement, but re-phrase your wording to prevent redundancy.

b). Write three to four sentences that re-mention all of your specific examples from your three body paragraphs. This section allows you to sum up your entire essay and reiterate your classification.

c). Provide one to two closing sentences.

Sample of a Conclusion:

(**a**) Although there are many ways that a person can classify his/her shoe collection, I like to categorize my shoes by work shoes, dress shoes, and exercise shoes. (**b**) My work shoes allow me to have a different pair for every day of the week, which is convenient in case one pair gets dirty. I love having my dress shoes in case there is an unexpected formal event, such as my cousin's wedding. Finally, I like having different exercise shoes for running and walking, such as Nike for walking and New Balance for running. (**c**) Classifying my shoe collection into three categories can be very beneficial.

Five-Paragraph Classification Essay Supplemental Information

How to Prewrite a Five-Paragraph Classification Essay

The classification essay will ask students to pick one object or element and divide it into three categories. This type of essay will fully explore those categories and explain them. This section will focus on prewriting the classification essay. Prewriting is an important step in the writing process, which helps students properly plan out their work in order to submit more successful essays. This section will teach college students how to prewrite a five-paragraph classification essay.

Step 1: Take time to think about the object or element that you want classify. Try to make sure that it is something that can be easily classified and divided. For example, you can classify your wardrobe into three categories. You can also divide a DVD collection into three categories. The point is that you will not want to pick a difficult topic; pick something that you know well.

Step 2: After picking the element that you will divide, try to make a minor list of possible categories that it can be divided into. Your essay will require three categories, so it is advised to make a list of at least six to seven things. The list will allow you to narrow down your categories into the three that you can write the most about.

Step 3: When you narrow down your list to three categories, try and do a free write or outline of these three categories. For the free write or outline, you will simply jot down your thoughts and main points about each category.

Step 4: Treat each category separately. Your main thoughts will include an explanation of each category, a specific example that illustrates your explanation, and other relevant information that you may include in your introduction.

Step 5: Take time to draft out your introduction, three body paragraphs and your conclusion. The best draft method is an outline. An outline will help you stay focused and organized with your thoughts and when you are writing the essay. The outline for your introduction will include general statements about the objects that you are dividing and a thesis statement of the three categories that you will divide your objects into. The body paragraphs will outline your explanations and examples of the three categories. Finally, the outline for you conclusion will summarize all of your main points from the introduction and body paragraphs.

How to Write a Thesis Statement for a Five-Paragraph Classification Essay

There are various genres of the five-paragraph essay. One type of five-paragraph essay is the classification essay. This type of essay asks students to pick one element and divide it up into categories. The classification essay helps students learn organizational skills. Furthermore, this type of essay teaches students that there are sub-categories to almost everything in life. As a result, the classification essay teaches students to become more analytical and observant of the world. This section provides step-by-step instructions and a few examples of how to write a thesis statement for a five-body paragraph classification essay.

Instructions for the Thesis Statement:

Step 1: The five-paragraph classification essay is composed of an introduction, three body paragraphs, and a conclusion. The introduction will discuss the element that the student is classifying. The introduction will also end with a one-sentence thesis statement that will divide the element into three categories. One body paragraph will be devoted to the three categories in your essay.

Step 2: Take time to think about the element that you want to write about, and make sure it is only one element for an essay this length. One element will allow you to have focus.

Step 3: Take time to think about three categories that your one element can be divided into, and make sure these categories all differ from each other. For example, you could classify your shirt collection into formal shirts, street shirts, and work shirts.

Step 4: Write one sentence that states the element you are writing about, and write three words or short phrases that describe the three categories that you will divide that element into. For example, you could write a thesis statement that says, "My DVD collection is classified into three categories, which are drama, horror, and action."

Step 5: Make sure your thesis statement is short and to the point before writing out your body paragraphs.

Sample thesis statements that work well for a five-paragraph classification essay:

Note: these are only samples, and your instructor may assign you different topics to write about. Either way, no matter what your topic is, these samples are what your thesis statement should look like.

1. I classify my DVD collection into horror films, action films, and drama films.

2. The cars at our college campus parking lot have three categories, which are sports cars, new cars, and beat up cars.

3. The cultures at my job consist of Hispanic, African, and Asian.

4. My father's liquor cabinet consists of beer, wine, and hard alcohol.

5. My sister has three types of shoes in her closet; they are dress shoes, ballet shoes, and work shoes.

How to Conclude a Five-Paragraph Classification Essay

This section will teach students how to conclude a five-paragraph classification essay.

Step One: Be sure that your introduction and three body paragraphs are fully developed. Your introduction will discuss the topic that is being classified, and your thesis will mention the three categories. Your body paragraphs will discuss the categories. Each body paragraph is devoted to each category. Your body paragraphs will contain an explanation of the category and provide a clear and specific example that illustrates your explanation.

Step Two: Begin writing your conclusion. Keep in mind that your conclusion will summarize your entire essay. It basically will re-cap all of your main points. Your conclusion needs to be developed and stick to your essay topic. Do not introduce new ideas in your conclusion. Again, re-mention all of your points from the essay.

Step Three: Write about two sentences that will re-mention your thesis statement. Your thesis is the last sentence of your introduction. Try to re-phrase your thesis in your conclusion to avoid repetitive sentence structure.

Step Four: In about four to five sentences, re-mention all of your explanations and specific examples from your three body paragraphs. This should be done briefly. Again, your conclusion only summarizes the main points of your entire essay.

Step Five: Close off your conclusion with about two intelligent thoughts regarding your overall topic. Again, do not introduce new information, as you will have to elaborate on that. Simply leave your reader with something to think about.

The Five-Paragraph Definition Essay

How to Write a Five-Paragraph Definition Essay

Most college freshmen will write a five-paragraph definition essay in their preparatory English classes. The definition essay asks students to pick one element in life that they are familiar with and define what that element means to them. The element that students will write about can be anything, such as friendship, a good parent, love, loss, hate, peace, war, sadness, happiness, etc. For this type of essay, students may refer to the dictionary to find a working definition of the element that they want to write about, but it is not necessary. This type of essay requires the student's definition. Each student will pick three defining key words or phrases for his/her element. This section will provide a step-by-step guideline and example to follow when writing the five-paragraph definition essay.

I. Recipe/Format for an Introduction:

a). Start your introduction with three to four general statements about the element that you are writing about. These statements can include the definition that is provided in the dictionary.

b). Provide about two sentences that show what your element may mean to other people.

c). Write a one sentence thesis statement that mentions the element that you will define, and be sure to have three defining key words or phrases that show what this element means to you.

Sample Introduction:

Note: The lower case letters are provided to illustrate the above format. These lower case letters will appear in all of the paragraph samples and formats.

(a) According to the Webster dictionary, the word, "home," means the place in which people reside. Home is the place where people and their loved ones live. Furthermore, a home is another word for a house. However, there is so much more to the word "home" than just the place where a person lives. **(b)** For some people, a home is truly where the heart is; it is a place where they feel content. For other people, the idea of a home is simply just the house where they live. **(c)** For me, the word "home" means a place of tranquility, a place that gives me identity, and a place where all of my loved ones are.

II. Recipe/Format for the 1st Body Paragraph:

a). Write two to three sentences that explain your first defining word from your thesis statement. Explain why this first key word/phrase defines your element.

b). Give a clear and specific three to four sentence example that portrays your first defining word/phrase. Your example can be about you, someone you know, or something you have read or seen. However, be sure to only pick one example.

c). Write one closing sentence.

Sample of the 1ˢᵗ Body Paragraph:

(a) I first believe that the idea of home means tranquility, and home does not just mean a house; it can mean the town where someone lives. When a person feels at home, he/she feels peace of mind. Every time people are in their home or home place, they feel like they are in their comfort zone, which brings tranquility. **(b)** For example, every time I leave my town to go into the city, I feel unsettled. People in the city are always nervous and rude; however, my hometown brings so much peace and relaxation to the people. Therefore, every time I return to my hometown, I feel a sense of tranquility and peace of mind. **(c)** The idea of home brings peace to many people.

III. Recipe/Format for the 2ⁿᵈ Body Paragraph:

a). Starting with a transitional phrase, write two to three sentences that explain your second defining word/phrase from your thesis.

b). Write another clear and specific example that illustrates your second explanation of your second key word/phrase. Again, this example should be about three to four sentences long.

c). Include one closing sentence.

Sample of the 2ⁿᵈ Body Paragraph:

(a) Second, the word, "home," means identity. For me the idea of home means identity because home is a place that shapes me and helps me become the person that I will become. My home is where I learn much about life and discover what is true for me and what is not true for me. **(b)** For instance, country/rock singer, John Mellencamp wrote and sung a song called, "Small Town." In this song, he discusses how this town is home to him and that it is a place that ultimately shaped him into the man he is today. This is a song about a hometown that constructs identity for this singer. **(c)** My home gives me identity.

IV. Recipe/Format for the 3ʳᵈ Body Paragraph:

a). Using another transitional phrase, explain your third defining key word/phrase in about two to three sentences. Again, tell why this word/phrase defines the topic that you are writing about.

b). Provide another clear and specific three to four sentence example, which supports your third explanation.

c). End your paragraph with one final sentence.

Sample of the 3rd Body Paragraph:

(**a**) Finally, home is a place where all of my loved ones live. When I have loved ones around, I feel at home. My loved ones provide comfort for me, and when I have comfort, I feel at peace, and when I feel at peace, I feel at home. (**b**) For example, all of my friends and family live in my hometown. When I am away from them, I feel so lost and lonely. When I am with these people, I always feel peace and content. We always barbeque together, and we have other types of gatherings together. When I am with them, I feel at home. (**c**) My loved ones create the idea of a home, and they make me feel at home.

V. Recipe/Format for a Conclusion:

a). In about one to two sentences and using different phrasing, re-state your thesis for your introduction.

b). Write about three to four sentences that re-cap all of your specific examples form your three body paragraphs.

c). Write one to two sentences that provide your reader with an intelligent thought about your overall topic.

Sample of a Conclusion:

(**a**) Although the idea of home means different things to many different people, for me, it means having tranquility, identity, and loved ones. These three elements define the meaning of home. (**b**) I always feel a sense of tranquility in my hometown; however, when I am in the city, I feel discomfort. As far as identity goes, John Mellencamp wrote a song called "Small Town," which articulates the notion of how a home constructs my identity. Finally, my loved ones always make me feel at home because we are always together having a great time and being happy. (**c**) The word "home," can mean my house; however, there is so much more to it than just a house. My home is truly where a person belongs.

The Five-Paragraph Definition Essay Supplemental Information

How to Write a Thesis Statement for a Five-Paragraph Definition Essay

The five-paragraph definition essay asks students to think of one element and define what that element means to them. The definition essay allows students to explore that one element in-depth. When the student picks the element and labels it with three defining words or phrases, he/she will devote a paragraph to each of those three words or phrases. Moreover, in order for the student to back up his or her definition, he/she needs to use specific examples in the body paragraphs. In order to let your reader know what your essay will discuss and define, it is important to have a clear and specific thesis statement at the end of your introduction. The thesis statement tells your reader exactly what your essay will discuss. This section will teach students how to write a thesis statement for a five-body paragraph definition essay, and it will also provide examples of various thesis statements.

Instructions for Writing a Thesis Statement:

Step 1: Take time to think about the element that you want to define. Remember, your element will not be something complicated. Make sure that it is something that everyone is familiar with. For example, you could write about what love, friendship, family, college, a good parent, a bad parent, etc. means to you. But for a five-paragraph essay, it is a good idea to pick only one element.

Step 2: Be sure that your thesis statement is the last sentence in your introduction. Everything above your thesis statement will be general ideas and general definitions of the element that you will be writing about.

Step 3: Write one sentence that states the element that you are going to write about, and make sure your sentence includes three words or phrases that tell what that element means to you. For example, if you are writing about friendship, you could write: "For me, friendship means being trustworthy, supportive, and giving." Notice how this one sentence states the element and has three defining words. One body paragraph will be devoted to each of those factors.

Step 4: Make sure that your thesis statement has three different defining key words. In other words, do not write three defining words that all mean the same thing. For example, do not write: "For me, friendship means loving, caring, and adoring." All of these words mean the same thing, and the point of this essay is to allow you to fully explore a topic. The same defining words will not allow you freedom to explore your thoughts.

Step 5: Make sure your thesis statement is clear and makes sense before you write out your body paragraphs.

Sample Thesis Statements for a Definition Essay:

Note: The following thesis statements are only samples, and your instructor may want you to define a particular topic. Either way, no matter what your topic is, your thesis statement for a five-paragraph definition essay should look just like the examples.

Sample Thesis Statement 1: For me, a loving relationship means having trust, humor, and communication.

Sample Thesis Statement 2: To me, friendship means being loyal, being giving, and being an open ear.

Sample Thesis Statement 3: Hating someone means anger, depression, and bitterness.

Sample Thesis Statement 4: When I take a vacation, it means that it time to relax, catch up on personal things, and spend time with loved ones.

Sample Thesis Statement 5: Owning a dog means companionship, entertainment, and responsibility.

These are only five sample thesis statements for a definition essay, but do notice there is a different style for each of them. As long as you write one clear, mechanically and grammatically correct English sentence, then you are free to choose your own style. However, do notice that all five styles are one sentence that mentions the element that will be defined, and notice that each sample thesis has three defining words or short phrases.

The Five-Paragraph Narration Essay

How to Write a Five-Paragraph Narration Essay

Most preparatory college English courses ask students to write a five-paragraph narration essay. The narration essay asks students to write about one life changing moment. This can be any kind of moment, such as sad, tragic, happy, funny, scary, etc. However, it must be a situation in your life that taught you something important and changed your life, and it must offer a moral or lesson to your reader. This type of essay allows students to re-live their past and find acceptance about that past; moreover, this type of essay teaches the reader how to articulate similar experiences or experiences that may come. This section will provide step-by-step instructions and examples for writing the five- paragraph narration essay.

I. Format/Recipe for an Introduction.

a) Write about two to three sentences that provide general discussion of your topic. Usually this section will provide a brief scenario or a series of questions relating to your topic.

b) Start your story with two to three sentences. Here you should mention the incident of the story and have an adjective that allows you to fully describe your emotions regarding that incident.

c) Write one to two sentences that state your thesis. Your thesis statement will provide the point of your story, the lesson that you learned, and/or how it changed you/your life.

Sample of an Introduction: The lower case letters in all the following sample paragraphs illustrate the formats/recipes for each paragraph. Use the lower case letters in all of the sample paragraphs as a checklist.

a) In America, the notion of divorce becomes more and more common. Many adults file for divorce, and when they do, they drag their children into the whole drama. When parents divorce, the children face much psychological turmoil. **b)** The saddest day of my life was when my parents got divorced. I always thought that my parents would be together. It was all the more sad because my dad did some things that provoked the ending of our happy family; he was having an affair. **c)** Although my mother, sister, and I had no choice but to say good-bye to our happy family, I learned that life will throw many uncontrollable situations at me, but I do have the power to control how I react when I face those situations. From this whole experience, I have learned to let go of self-blame and to take responsibility for my own actions.

II. Format/Recipe for the 1st Body Paragraph:

a) Write about two to three sentences that tell how your story began; discuss the first incident of your narrative. Ask yourself, "What was the first fragment or moment in my story?"

b) In about three to four sentences, illustrate your emotions regarding your incident. Tell everything that went through your mind during this time. In order to show the reader how you felt, be sure to compare your thoughts and emotions to various objects.

c) Seal off your paragraph with one to two closing sentences.

Sample of the 1st Body Paragraph:

a) I was twelve years old when my parents divorced. I will never forget the day we discovered that my father was having an affair with his secretary. My mom and I were out shopping, while my dad and sister were home. When he was on the phone, my sister overheard my father's conversation with his mistress. When my sister told my mom, we all confronted him. At first he denied it, but then he confessed. **(b)** Before this day, we were happy; my parents were married for 20 years, so when the word "divorce" was mentioned, I knew life would change forever. My thoughts became pieces of shattered glass. I felt lost, scared, sad, confused; I felt worse than hearing the sounds of a thousand fingernails scraping against a black chalkboard. **(c)** I felt these emotions because I knew my identity was not solid; it was easily shattered. My family was my identity; therefore, my father shattered that identity.

III. Format/Recipe for the 2nd Body Paragraph.

a) Starting with a transitional phrase, write about three to four more sentences that discuss the second important detail. Simply discuss the next incident or phase of your narrative.

b) In about three to four sentences, discuss another example of the thoughts that ran through your mind; discuss your emotions. Remember to portray your emotions by making comparisons to various objects.

c) Write one to two closing sentences to end your paragraph.

Sample of the 2nd Body Paragraph:

a). After the fiasco of confronting my father, my parents discussed separating. My mother wanted my father to leave, but he would not. My father decided to let months pass in silence. He stayed in the house, we stayed in the house, and he continued his life. My mother, sister, and I lived like zombies for months, never discussing the affair. My dad would go to work and come home as if nothing happened. **(b)** A change occurred, a dent, a scar. I remember thinking that I should have been a better son. Was it my fault? The shattered mirror image of myself poked away at my mind; I should have been a better son. My own mind became my own prison. I wanted to be free. I wanted to go back to the way things used to be. I wanted to tell myself it was not my fault, but I could not. My father took that chance from me, from us. **(c)** My father was my best friend and the only one who I could be free with and be just me, and I was scared to lose him.

IV. Format/Recipe for the 3rd Body Paragraph:

a) Write about two to three sentences that discuss the third major incident of your narrative.

b) Just as you did for your first and second body paragraph, write three to four more sentences that fully illustrate your thoughts and emotions. Again, paint a picture of your emotions by using words. You should compare your thoughts and emotions to various objects.

c) Write one to two closing sentences that will allow you to seal off your paragraph.

Sample of the 3rd Body Paragraph:

(a) After months of silence, my father moved out, and my mother, sister, and I stayed in the house. We stayed in the house temporally because my father stopped paying for everything, so we moved to an apartment, while my father bought another home with his secretary. My father did not want us in his life. While living in the apartment, my mother, sister, and I began the healing process. **(b)** Saying goodbye to my father and to our house was the hardest part of the divorce. For about four years, my mom, sister, and I tried to carry on with our lives that best way we that we could, but it was not easy. We all faced much anger, blame, and self-blame. I could not feel anything. My thoughts and emotions were a spiral of an endless tornado. I went from Marteen to Martin. Can I ever get back to being Marteen, or am I stuck Martin? Or can I be both? Each day, I was further losing myself, while my father was off finding himself. **(c)** For the first time, I felt what it was like to not feel. There was no going back to the way things used to be.

V. Format/Recipe for a Conclusion

a) Write two to three sentences that tell how your story ends. Discuss how you were able to move on to the next phase of your life.

b) In about three to four sentences, re-mention all of your main points or the three phases that you went through during your narrative.

c) In about four to five sentences, close your narrative with the lesson that you learned and how you changed as a person. Also, offer a moral or piece of advice to your reader.

Sample of a Conclusion:

(a) After years and years of self-blame, I dropped out of high school, and started to hang out with the wrong crowd, and my sister went to college. However, my mother never gave up on me, and I will always love her. I decided to get my high school diploma and start college. In college, I met a mentor, a father figure, who taught me everything that I now know about reading, writing, and life. **(b)** While in college, I thought about the past. I thought about the first moment that we found out my father was having an affair and how it made me feel. I thought about the four months of silence and how I was so scared of losing my dad. I thought about the apartment and the anger that we all faced, and I thought about how it is time to let go of my self-blame. **(c)** Now, I think about my schooling, and I know that it is time to face the past, have a responsible acceptance of that past, and let go of that past in order to love my present and embrace the future. If anyone ever is a victim of divorce, it is hard, but it is important to know that no one and nothing controls us. We control ourselves. It is important to know that divorce is never your fault, and it does not mean life is over; it means that life is just beginning.

The Five-Paragraph Narration Essay Supplemental Information

How to Prewrite a Five-Paragraph Narrative Essay

Most college English courses will ask their students to write a narrative essay. This type of essay asks students to relive one life changing moment and write about it. For this type of essay, students are to pick the moment or incident and pick an adjective that describes the incident. Students are to fully explore their moment, tell what happened, and describe their emotions regarding that incident. The narrative essay allows students to face the past and form an acceptance of that past. This type of essay can also teach the reader a lesson about how to deal with a similar experience. Because this type of essay can be challenging, it is important to prewrite. This type of an essay can be challenging because facing the past is not easy. Prewriting will help develop and organize your thoughts. This section will teach college students how to prewrite a narrative essay.

Step 1: Take time to meditate and think about a significant moment in your life. While you are meditating, think about that one moment, and try to relive it to the fullest. Think about what happened and how it impacted your life. Think about your thoughts and emotions. While you are thinking about this, it is a good idea to close your eyes and take deep breaths in and out. Try this exercise in a place where you will not be disturbed. This type of exercise will allow you to clear your mind and focus on the incident that you want to write about.

Step 2: When you are done meditating, do a free write. Simply write down your thoughts in a stream of consciousness way. Do not worry about proper sentence structure, organization, or development. The free write is designed to simply allow your thoughts to flow openly and freely. The free write will help loosen your mind, and your words will come out honestly and truthful.

Step 3: After the free write, do an outline of your essay. In the outline, you can simply arrange the order of your story. It is best to organize your outline in a chronological order. In other words, you should simply arrange your story in the order that the events occurred. Your outline should list out your main ideas, the events, and your emotions of the events. The outline will help you write a fully developed essay. The outline will help you organize your introduction, thesis statement, body paragraphs and your conclusion.

How to Write a Thesis Statement for a Five-Body Paragraph Narration Essay

The five-paragraph narration essay asks students to re-live one fragment or experience from their lives. Moreover, the narration essay asks students to write about the events that took place during that time of their life and describe the thoughts and emotions about that experience. The narration allows students to face their own past and articulate their thoughts and emotions about that past. The narration essay is a great therapeutic tool for students and all writers because it allows writers to face the past and responsibly accept that past. This type of writing asks the writer to tell a lesson or moral that was learned. The thesis statement of the narration will offer a point of the story and a moral to the reader. This section will teach students how to construct a solid thesis statement for the five-paragraph narration essay. Furthermore, this section will provide a few sample narration thesis statements.

Instructions for Writing a Narrative Thesis Statement:

Step 1: Take time to think of the story that you want to write about. The narration essay asks students to think of a life-changing situation to write about.

Step 2: After thinking about the situation and constructing your introduction, be sure to think about the point or moral that you are trying to convey to your reader. Your point will be the lesson you learned and some advice for your reader.

Step 3: After thinking of your overall point, write one to two sentences that state your thesis at the end of your introduction. Make sure that this thesis statement states the incident of your story, and the lesson that you learned, and that lesson should offer a moral or piece of advice to your reader.

Step 4: After writing out your thesis statement, make sure that it flows smoothly and makes sense.

Sample Thesis Statements for a Five-Paragraph Narration Essay:

Note: There are endless stories to tell and to re-live. Some stories are sad, happy, funny, tragic, scary, traumatizing, etc. No matter what type of story you narrate, your thesis statement should look like the following samples.

Sample Thesis Statement 1: Although my parents' divorce was the saddest time of my life, I learned that many sad things happen to people, and it is important to not let the sad moments of the past hold people back from enjoying the happy ones of the present and future.

Sample Thesis Statement 2: When my best friend died, I thought my life was over; however, with time, I learned that death is inevitable, and my friend would not want me to live like I was dead too.

Sample Thesis Statement 3: My wedding day was the happiest day of my life, and from that day, I learned that happy moments do not happen all the time, so it is important to enjoy them and embrace them when they do happen.

The above sample thesis statements offer different emotions and different story topics; however, do notice that all three samples state the incident of the story, the lesson that was learned, and a moral that can be passed down to the reader.

How to Write an Introduction for a Narrative Essay

The narrative essay asks students to tell a personal story. For the most part, this type of an essay asks students to re-live one life changing moment. This type of an essay can be emotionally challenging because students will revisit a moment in their lives that they may have forgotten about. This type of an essay will allow students to re-examine their emotions and feelings regarding their past experience. In this section, I will provide instructions that will teach students how to write an introduction for a narrative essay. There will also be a sample introduction.

Step1: Before you begin writing, it is important to take some time to think about your life. Take time to relive the most significant and life changing moments. Take time to narrow your life down to one of the most impacting moments. For example, if your parents went through a divorce, then this is certainly a life changing moment for you as the child. This is one incident that you can write about.

Step 2: Begin your narration with four to five general statements regarding the topic that you are writing about. These opening lines are not your story; it is simply a general overview of your topic. For example, if you are writing about the death of a relative, then you may simply open your essay with a few general statements about how people lose their loved ones. This statements can be "what if" questions or general scenarios.

Step 3: The second part of your introduction will mention your topic. This part should be done in about one to two sentences. In this section of your introduction, you will state your incident and have an adjective that describes the incident. For example, "The saddest day of my life was when my parents got a divorce." The word "saddest" is the adjective that describes the incident, and "when my parents got a divorce" is the incident.

Step 4: The final part of your introduction will be your thesis statement. The thesis statement for this type of an essay should be about two to three sentences long. Your thesis statement will provide your reader with the overall point or moral of your story. It will discuss how you overcame or are overcoming your past experience and the lessons that you learned. It is important that your thesis statement contains this information because you cannot tell a story without a point or moral.

Sample Introduction:

Everybody has experienced a relationship at one time or another. Moreover, everyone has experienced a breakup. Perhaps breakups are one of the most painful things that a person can deal with. In fact, I compare a breakup to the death of a loved one. When someone goes through a breakup, he/she does lose a loved one. The hardest time in my life was when my girlfriend of five years broke up with me. I was hard because I truly loved her, and I did not see it coming. Although this was a challenging time in my life and felt that I could not go on, I learned one valuable lesson. In life, there will be surprises. Some of those surprises may be bad ones, but even with the bad surprises, life is a continuing journey, and it is important to keep moving forward to experience the good surprises too.

How to Write the Body Paragraphs for a Narrative Essay

The narrative essay asks students to relive a life changing experience. For this type of an essay, students are to discuss the incident, show how it changed them, and make the reader feel exactly what the writer felt at the time. This type of an essay teaches students how to relive the past and embrace that past for a more healthy perspective of the present and future. This section will teach students how to write the body paragraphs for a narrative essay.

Step 1: Your narrative essay should contain at least three fully developed and well-organized body paragraphs. These paragraphs are to perform the following functions. Each body paragraph should discuss each major event that occurred in your incident. For example, if you are writing about an accident that you experienced, then your first body paragraph will discuss the events that led up to the accident, the second body paragraph will discuss the events that happened during the accident, and the third body paragraphs will discuss the events that happened after the accident. Your body paragraphs should also make the reader feel exactly what you felt like at the time.

Step 2: In about four to five sentences, it is a good idea to open each paragraph with a description or discussion of each event that occurred in your incident. Each discussion should simply tell what happened first, second, and third. Be detailed in your discussion and tell the story in a to-the-point manner. Do not circle around each event; simply jump right into it.

Step 3: After discussing each event and telling what happened, it is important to hold your readers' attention. The best way to hold your readers' attention is to make your reader feel exactly what you felt at the time. The best way to make your reader feel what you felt is to compare your thoughts and emotions to various objects. When you make comparisons, it adds depth and richness to your writing. Be sure that you show your reader exactly what was in your mind. This should be done in about four to five sentences.

Step 4: End each paragraph with one or two closing sentences. These sentences should simply seal off your paragraphs. Do not leave your paragraphs open. The best way to seal off your paragraphs is to simply provide a final thought regarding each event.

How to Conclude a Narrative Essay

In short, the narrative essay teaches students how to relive a past experience. Furthermore, this type of essay allows students to form a responsible acceptance of that past in order to live a healthier and more fulfilling present and future. In fact, this type of writing is very therapeutic, and it allows students to fully understand their past and embrace their emotions and feelings about that past. This section will teach college student show to conclude a narrative essay.

Step 1: Unlike most essays, this type of conclusion does not necessarily summarize all of the main points from your essay introduction and essay body. For the narrative essay, you are concluding your past experience. In short, you will tell your reader how your story ends. If the incident that you are writing about has not fully ended, then you can simply tell your reader what you are attempting to do to move on to the next phase of your life.

Step 2: Begin your conclusion with about three to four sentences that tell your reader how your story ends. Tell your reader about the final major event in your incident. In most essays, you will begin your introduction with a re-cap of your thesis statement. For this type of an essay, it is only necessary to begin your conclusion with how your story ends.

Step 3: After telling how your story ends, be sure to re-mention all of the major events that you explore in your body paragraphs. For this section, you can re-mention your thesis statement if you choose to, but it is not mandatory. However, it is a good idea to summarize all that you went through during your incident. Again, the major events of your story will appear in your body paragraphs. This should all be done in about three to four sentences.

Step 4: End you conclusion with the overall moral of your story and/or the lesson that you will take with you for the rest of your life. You should also end your conclusion with a piece of advice for your reader. The piece of advice should regard the incident that you wrote about. This should all be done in about two to three sentences.

Five-Paragraph Compare and Contrast Essay

How to Write a Five-Paragraph Compare and Contrast Essay

The five-paragraph compare and contrast essay will be written by most college freshmen in their preparatory English classes. For this type of essay, students will examine the similarities and the differences between two elements or objects. For the most part, students will discuss three similarities between the two elements/objects that they write about, and they will spend the majority of their essay examining the differences between those similarities. This section will provide a step-by-step guideline and an example of a fully developed and well-organized five-paragraph compare and contrast essay.

Note: When writing your own essay, follow this format as you would a cooking recipe. All of the following ingredients should be in your own body paragraphs. Furthermore, I provide the lower case letters in the sample paragraphs to illustrate the paragraph recipe/formats.

I. Recipe/Format for an Introduction:

a). Write about two to three general statements regarding your topic. These sentences/statements should provide a general idea of what you will be comparing and contrasting.

b). In about two sentences mention some of the things that people would compare and contrast regarding the topic that you will be writing about.

c). Write a one to two sentence thesis statement that includes three similarities between your two objects. This thesis statement should also mention the three differences within those similarities.

Sample of an Introduction:

(a) Many college students take two classes that deal with the same subject during a semester, and they will have two different professors. For example, some students may take two math classes in a semester with two different instructors. Furthermore, some students may take two English classes with two different professors. **(b)** If these students have two different professors, they may compare and contrast their teaching techniques. Other students may compare and contrast the two professors' personalities. **(c)** Both of my English professors give a lot of reading, are strict with essay guidelines, and have exciting class sessions. However, one professor assigns boring reading, is more strict with grammar over content/organization, and one professor is exciting with lectures, while the other is exciting with class discussion.

II. Recipe/Format for a 1st Body Paragraph:

a). In two to three sentences, discuss the first similarity and the difference within that similarity between your two elements/objects.

b). Write three to four sentences that give a clear and specific example of the difference between your two subjects. Make sure this example illustrates the difference between your two subjects.

c). End your paragraph with one closing sentence.

Sample of a 1st Body Paragraph:

(a) First of all, both of my English professors assign a lot of reading. However, my British literature professor assigns much literature, which I find boring and dry, and it puts me to sleep. On the other hand, my American literature professor assigns some really exciting literature. **(b)** For example, in my British literature course, we had to read Virginia Woolf's *To the Lighthouse*, which had no entertainment at all; it was dry and slow moving. However, in my American literature class, we had to read Mark Twain's **Huck Finn**. This novel was filled with action, humor, and suspense. I did not get bored reading it. **(c)** Both classes have a lot of reading, but one reading is more fun than the other.

III. Recipe/Format for a 2nd Body Paragraph:

a). Using a transitional phrase, write two to three sentences that explain the second similarity and difference between your two subjects. This explanation will be set up the same way as body paragraph one.

b). In about three to four sentences, provide an illustrative, clear, and specific example of the difference between your two objects/elements.

c). Seal off your paragraph with one closing sentence.

Sample of a 2nd Body Paragraph:

(a) Another similarity between both of my two English professors is that they are both strict with their grading/writing guidelines. However, my British literature professor is very strict with grammar, while my American literature professor focuses on content and organization. **(b)** For instance, when I turned in my first essay, my British literature professor marked it up with fragment sentences, run-ons, subject-verb agreement errors, word choice errors, wordiness, etc., and there was no feedback with content/organization. However, my first essay from my American literature class had only content and organization mark ups and no grammar. When I looked at both of my first essays, I had the same mistakes on both of them, grammatically and content wise, but they both only showed one type of feedback. **(c)** Either way, both professors have strict writing guidelines.

IV. Recipe/Format for a 3rd Body Paragraph:

a). Start with a transitional phrase and write about two to three sentences that explain your third similarity and difference between your two subjects.

b). Just as you did for body paragraphs one and two, give another specific example that illustrates the third difference. Remember that your example should only be about two to three sentences long.

c). Write one closing sentence.

Sample of a 3rd Body Paragraph:

(a) Finally, both of my English professors hold exciting class sessions. However, my British literature professor only provides exciting lecture with a lot of enthusiasm; he is hyper. On the other hand, my American literature professor holds really great class discussion; he involves the class and always asks for our thoughts and opinions on the reading. **(b)** To illustrate, although my British literature reading list is boring, my professor always provides great historical and contextual knowledge, and he says a lot of funny jokes between his lectures. He did this for our lecture on Woolf's *To the Lighthouse*. On the other hand, my American literature professor engaged all of us in class discussion when we read *Huck Finn*. We all shared great thoughts that allowed us to give each other perspective on the novel. This made class entertaining. **(c)** I love the class sessions in both of my classes.

V. Recipe/Format for a Conclusion:

a). In about two sentences, re-state your thesis from your introduction, but try to use different phrasing.

b). Re-mention all of your specific examples from your three body paragraphs in about three to four sentences.

c). Seal off your entire essay with one to two closing sentences about your overall topic.

Sample of a Conclusion:

(a) Although both of my professors have a lot of reading, strict grading tactics, and exciting class sessions, my British literature professor assigns boring reading, grades primarily on grammar, and he gives exciting lectures. My American literature professor has a fun reading list, grades on content and organization, and engages all of us in class discussion. **(b)** For example, *To the Lighthouse* was boring, and *Huck Finn* was exciting. My British literature essays are always marked with grammar errors, while my

American literature essays always have feedback on content and organization. Finally, I love my British literature professor's jokes during lecture, and I love how my American literature professor engages the class in discussions. **(c)** Both of my English professors may have similarities, but they are both very different. However, one thing that they do have in common is that they are both great professors.

The Five-Paragraph Compare and Contrast Supplemental Information

How to Prewrite a Five Paragraph Compare and Contrast Essay

The compare and contrast essay asks students to pick two objects and distinguish the similarities and the differences. These objects can be anything, such as two people, two places, two things, etc. For the purposes of this discussion, this section will provide information that will teach college students how to prewrite the compare and contrast essay. Prewriting is an important part of the writing process because it helps students organize and develop their thoughts.

Step 1: Take time to think about two things that you want to compare and contrast. It is important to make a list of the similarities of these two objects. It is also important to make a list of differences between these two objects. The list will help you to organize your thoughts and begin arranging the similarities and differences in a more suitable way.

Step 2: Try to narrow down your thoughts to three similarities and three differences within those similarities or vice versa. For example, you could say that your two best friends are smart, funny, and hyper; however, one is smart in school, while the other is street smarts. Furthermore, one friend has clean jokes, and the other is vulgar. Finally, one is only hyper after caffeine and the other is naturally hyper.

Step 3: If the narrowing down process is not working out after the list, then do a Venn diagram. The Venn diagram is simply two overlapping circles. In one end of the circle, you write down a few descriptive words about one object. In the other end of the circle, you simply write down a few descriptive words about the other object. In the middle of the circles, you simply write down the similarities between both objects. This is an effective technique for the compare and contrast essay.

Step 4: Finally, do a free write of the essay or an outline. The outline will simply list all of your main ideas for each body paragraph. The outline will help you organize what you want to explore in the actual essay. For the outline, you only need to list short phrases or sentences of your main ideas in each paragraph. For example, in your introduction, you can list your two objects and your thesis statement, which is the compare and contrast that you will explore in your essay body.

How to Write a Thesis Statement for Five-Paragraph Compare and Contrast Essay

The five-paragraph compare and contrast essay asks students to examine the similarities and the differences between two objects. Moreover, the compare and contrast essay asks students to write about three similarities between two objects and then contrast those similarities. This type of essay helps students become more analytical when it comes to writing about two objects. The thesis statement at the end of the introduction tells the reader exactly what element you will be comparing and contrasting. Moreover, the thesis statement will tell your reader the three similarities and the distinct differences within those similarities. This section will teach students how to write a nice and clear thesis statement for the five-paragraph compare and contrast essay. This section will also provide sample thesis statements for a compare and contrast essay.

Instructions for a Compare and Contrast Thesis Statement:

Step 1: Take some time to think about the two elements that you want to compare and contrast. For this type of essay it is good to write about two things that are compatible with each other. For example, you could write about two best friends, two horror films, two twins, two houses, etc.

Step 2: When it comes time to write the thesis statement, make sure that you write one to two sentences that present the two elements that you are comparing and contrasting.

Step 3: When you write this thesis that presents your two elements, make sure that you mention three things that show similarity between these two elements. For example, you could write: "My two best friends are tall, smart, and funny."

Step 4: Now that you have written the three similarities, be sure that you also write three distinct differences within those similarities. Writing the differences within those similarities will give your paper full focus. For example, you could write: "My two best friends are tall, smart and funny; however, one friend is lanky, while the other is normally tall; furthermore, one friend uses his brain, while the other does not apply himself; and finally, one friend tells classic jokes, and the other tells demented jokes."

Step 5: Make sure your thesis is clear, makes sense, tells your two elements, and shows the three similarities and/or the three differences.

Step 6: Your thesis statement can also have one big similarity and three distinct differences, but be sure that if you do choose this, then you write about something that is highly compatible, such as two small dogs.

Sample Compare and Contrast Thesis Statements:
Note: No matter what topic you write about or are instructed to write about, the following examples are how your thesis statement should look.

Sample Thesis Statement 1: My two best friends are tall, smart, and funny; however, one friend is lanky, while the other is normally tall. Furthermore, one friend uses his brain, while the other does not apply himself, and one friend tells classic jokes, and the other tells demented jokes.

Sample Thesis Statement 2: My parents have two houses, which are both big, spacious, and have swimming pools; however, one house is a two story and the other is not; in addition, one house has spacious bedrooms, while the other only has a spacious living room; and last, one house has a huge swimming pool, while the other is small.

Sample Thesis Statement 3: My girlfriend has two small dogs; however, one is mean, and the other is nice; furthermore, one is smart, while the other one is dumb; and finally, one is hyper, while the other is lazy.

Notice that the above example thesis statements all contain the two elements that will be compared and contrasted. Also, all thesis statements show the similarities and the differences within those similarities.

How to Write the Body Paragraphs for the Five-Paragraph Compare and Contrast Essay

This section will teach students how to construct and write the body paragraphs for a compare and contrast essay. This section will show students how to write the body paragraphs that 100% support their thesis statement. Moreover, this section will provide sample body paragraphs for the five-paragraph compare and contrast essay.

Instructions for Writing the Three Body Paragraphs for a Compare and Contrast Essay:

Step One: Be sure to look at your thesis statement and focus on the three similarities between your two elements. While focusing on the three similarities, pay close attention the three differences within those similarities. For example, if two friends are funny, perhaps the difference between their humor is that one friend tells nasty jokes, while the other tells clean jokes. Notice the similarity that both friends are funny, but they contrast because they are funny in different ways.

Step Two: Body paragraph one will be devoted to one similarity and the difference within that similarity, body paragraph two will be devoted to the second similarity and the difference within that similarity, and body paragraph three will be devoted to the third similarity and the difference within that similarity. All three similarities and differences will appear in your thesis statement.

Step Three: For body paragraph one, write one to two sentences that state the first similarity and difference from your thesis. Next, write three to four sentences that provide a specific example that explain and illustrate the difference between the similarity. Finally, end with one closing sentence for body paragraph one.

Step Four: For body paragraph two, write one to two sentences that state the second similarity and difference from your thesis. Second, write three to four sentences that provide a specific example that will allow you to illustrate the second difference within the second similarity. Finally, end with one closing sentence.

Step Five: For body paragraph three, write one to two sentences that state the third similarity and difference from you thesis statement. Next, write three to four sentences that illustrate your third difference regarding your third similarity. Write one closing sentence to seal off this paragraph.

Step Six: Make sure all three-body paragraphs clearly state the similarities and the differences within those similarities. Make sure that all body paragraphs have a clear and specific example that explains and illustrates those differences, and make sure all body paragraphs have a closing sentence.

Samples:

Note: No matter what you are comparing and contrasting, your body paragraphs should look similar to the following samples.

Sample Thesis Statement: Both Stockton, CA. and Lodi, CA. have rich neighborhoods, ghettos, and great restaurants; however, Stockton has more snobs in the rich neighborhoods than Lodi, Stockton's ghettos are more dangerous than Lodi's, and Stockton has more variety of international restaurants while Lodi is limited.

Sample Body Paragraph 1: First of all, Stockton and Lodi both have rich neighborhoods. However, Stockton has many more snobs in those neighborhoods than Lodi. For example, every time my friends and I walk or jog in those neighborhoods in Stockton, we will say hello to people who are also walking or jogging, and they simply give us the cold shoulder. On the other hand, every time we are in the rich neighborhoods in Lodi, people always say hello and are friendly. Those are the differences between the rich neighborhoods in Stockton and Lodi.

Sample Body Paragraph 2: Another similarity between Stockton and Lodi is that they both have ghettos. However, The ghettos in Stockton are much more dangerous than Lodi. For instance, there are shootings in the ghettos of Stockton reported almost every day in the evening news or the morning newspaper. On the other hand, very little crime is reported from the ghettos of Lodi, other than a robbery every so often. Both towns have ghettos, but one is more dangerous than the other.

Sample Body Paragraph 3: Finally, both towns have great restaurants, but Stockton has more of a variety of international restaurants than Lodi. To illustrate, Stockton has a variety of Chinese, Japanese, Mexican, Indian, Thai, Italian, and American restaurants. On the other hand, Lodi only has one or two of each kind of restaurant. In fact, Lodi has only one Indian and Thai restaurant and a handful of other types of cuisines. As you can see, both towns have great restaurants, but Stockton has many more to choose from than Lodi.

Notice how all body paragraphs show the similarities, but fully explain and illustrate the differences within those similarities by using specific examples. Also, each body paragraph has a closing sentence.

The Five-Paragraph Illustration Essay

How to Write a Five-Paragraph Illustration Essay

In most college preparatory English courses, students will be asked to write a five-paragraph illustration essay. This kind of an essay requires students to use reasons and examples to explain their topic. Students are usually asked to discuss one object or element that they know well and illustrate why they like or dislike it. The object or element that students can write about can be a place, person, or thing. This section will provide step-by-step instructions that will teach students how to write a fully developed and well-organized five-paragraph illustration essay. This section will also provide students with a sample of each paragraph, which will illustrate the paragraph formats.

Note: Be sure to follow each guideline/format as you would a cooking recipe. Make sure that all the ingredients are in your own paragraphs.

I. Recipe/Format for an Introduction:

a). Write two to three sentences that provide a general discussion of your topic. These sentences should generalize the topic that you will be discussing.

b). Provide two sentences that show what others think about the topic that you are writing about.

c). Write one thesis statement. Your thesis statement should be one sentence that tells why you either like or dislike the object that you are writing about. You need to also include three clear and specific reasons why you either like or dislike your object.

Sample of an Introduction:

Note: The lower case letters are designed to illustrate the paragraph recipe/formats.

(a) Many college students use the library for a number of reasons. Although college libraries are designed for students to study, many students end up using them to just hang out or kill time before their next class. Moreover, many students use their college library to check out free books to read or to research for their class projects. **(b)** Despite all these reasons to use the library, there are many students who dislike studying at their college library. On the other hand, there are many students who love studying at the college library. **(c)** I personally love studying at my college library because it is quiet, other people are around, and all of my resources are there.

II. Recipe/Format for Your 1st Body Paragraph:

a). In about two to three sentences, give one explanation of your first reason from you thesis statement.

b). With three to four sentences, provide your reader with a clear and specific example that illustrates your first explanation.

c). Write one closing sentence.

Sample of Body Paragraph One:

(a) I first love studying at my college library because it is quiet. I do my best studying when it is quiet with no distractions. I never hear anyone talking in our college library. **(b)** For example, one day I had a huge exam to study for, but my home was really noisy with my family. I tried studying at a coffee house, and the noise was no better; I could not focus. Therefore, I went to my quiet college library, and I was able to study peacefully. I ended up with an "A" on my exam the following week. **(c)** If I would not have studied at my library, then chances are I would not have been able to focus and pass my exam.

III. Recipe/Format for Your 2nd Body Paragraph:

a). Just as you did for body paragraph one, write two to three sentences that explain your second reason from your thesis. However, do start with a transitional phrase.

b). Write three to four sentences that give another clear and specific example, which will portray your explanation for the reader.

c). Seal off your paragraph with one closing sentence.

Sample of Body Paragraph Two:

(a) Furthermore, I love studying at my college library because there are other people around. Study time can be lonely time, so when I see other people around doing the same thing as me, it eases the tension. Also, when I need a break from studying, there are other people who I can talk with outside. **(b)** To illustrate, I used to study at my home when no one was around. When I did this, I felt very depressed and lonely. However, the first day I studied at my library, I saw people studying all over. Furthermore, that same day, I needed a break and was able to visit with a classmate outside for a while. We laughed about various topics. The laughter made it easier to go back and study. **(c)** I love studying at my library because it is not lonely and depressing.

IV. Recipe/Format for Your 3rd Body Paragraph:

a). Explain your third reason from your thesis in about two to three sentences and start with a transitional phrase.

b). Write another example that supports your third explanation. Again, your example should be three to four sentences long.

c). Provide one final sentence to seal of your third body paragraph.

Sample of Body Paragraph Three:

(a) Finally, I love studying at my college library because it has all of my resources. Whenever I am studying, I always find that I need further references or research material. Therefore, if I ever need clarification or further material regarding a specific topic, I can simply search all of the library databases for books and/or articles. **(b)** For example, last semester, I was assigned to write a research paper about a subject that I knew nothing about. Well, at the library, I was able to read up on my topic and gather all the information from the library. I got an "A" on my paper. **(c)** If it was not for the library, then I would not have found the proper resources for my paper topic.

V. Recipe/Format for a Conclusion:

a). In about two sentences, re-mention your thesis statement from your introduction. Make sure that you use different phrasing.

b). Re-mention your specific examples from your three body paragraphs in about three to four sentences, so that you can reiterate your thesis statement.

c). Write one to two closing sentences that provide your overall thoughts regarding the topic that you wrote about.

Sample of a Conclusion:

(a) Although there are many reasons to study at the library, I love to study at our college library because of how quiet it is. I also love my college library because there are people around who are doing the same thing as me. Also, it contains many helpful resources. **(b)** If I would not have had the peace and quiet that I get at the library, I would have failed my exam and other exams. Furthermore, I love taking breaks from studying by talking to other people who are at the library. I also was able to write a successful research paper from the resources at our college library. **(c)** As my reader can see, these are the three reasons why I love to study at my college library.

The Five-Paragraph Illustration Essay Supplemental Information

How to Prewrite a Five-Paragraph Illustrative Essay

The illustrative essay asks students to use reasons and examples in their writing. The examples, which will appear in the body paragraphs, are one of the things that will make this type of an essay stand strong. Most preparatory college English courses will ask that their students write a five-paragraph illustrative essay. This section will focus on prewriting this type of an essay. Prewriting is an important part of the writing process, which helps students organize and develop their thoughts for the final draft of the essay. This section will teach college students how to prewrite an illustrative essay.

Step 1: This type of essay might ask students to explain why they like or dislike a particular place, person, or thing. The students will need to provide three reasons why they feel the way they do, and they will need to provide illustrative examples that support their reasons. Therefore, take time to think about the person, place, or thing that you want to write about. Students are usually free to choose their topic. For example, you can choose to write about three reasons why you like the beach.

Step 2: After choosing your topic, try to pick three reasons why you either like or dislike the topic. It is best to write out a list of the pros and cons. Whichever list is bigger is probably the better choice to write about. For example, if your pros list is bigger, it means that you like the person, place, or thing that you are writing about; therefore, it will be easier for you to focus. Next, narrow down your list to three reasons that you feel you will be able to write the most about.

Step 3: When you have your three reasons, take time to either free write or outline specific examples that will illustrate your reasons. The examples will allow you to show your reader what you mean and why you feel the way you do. The reasons and explanations will only tell your reader, but the examples will show your reader. The free write or outline can simply list the specifics. For example, if you dislike the beach, and one of your reasons is because it is sandy, then you can provide an example of a day that you were on the beach and all the sand stuck to you. Be specific with the examples.

Step 4: Finally, take time to outline your introduction, three body paragraphs, and conclusion. The outline will simply list all of your main and supporting ideas for each paragraph. For example, your introduction will list your thesis statement, which will provide your three reasons. Your body paragraphs will list your explanations and specific examples. The conclusion will list main points from the overall essay.

How to Write a Thesis Statement for a Five-Paragraph Illustration Essay

This five-paragraph illustration essay asks students to write about a particular element and provide reasons and examples about the element. The illustration essay allows students to think deeply about the topic that they are writing about. Furthermore, this type of essay allows students to communicate their knowledge to the reader. The specific reasons and examples that this essay requires allow the students to communicate this knowledge. At the end of the introduction, students will write one thesis statement that tells the reader three reasons why the writer feels a certain way about a particular issue. This section will teach students how to write a thesis statement for a five-paragraph illustration essay. Furthermore, this section will provide sample thesis statements for this type of an essay.

Instructions for Writing an illustration Thesis Statement:

Step 1: Take some time to think about the topic that you are writing about, and think of the reasons that you want to write about the topic. For this type of essay, it is usually best to just think of something you either like or dislike.

Step 2: Take some time to think about 3 reasons that will allow you to illustrate your topic. Your reasons should explain to the reader why you feel the way you do about a certain issue.

Step 3: At the end of your introduction, write one sentence, which provides three words or short phrases that give reasons for your topic. In other words, make sure that your three words or phrases explain your thoughts about the topic that you are writing about.

Step 4: Make sure your thesis statement is one sentence, clearly stated, which contains the main topic of your essay, and has three reasons of explanation.

Sample Illustration Thesis Statements:

Sample Thesis Statement 1: I love walking because it keeps me relaxed, healthy, and thin.

Sample Thesis Statement 2: My favorite place to study is the library because it is quiet, it has many resources, and people are around.

Sample Thesis Statement 3: I do not like violent films because there is too much sadness in real life, they create hostility, and they are too bloody.

Sample Thesis Statement 4: I love writing because it allows me to escape, communicate my thoughts, and improve my thinking.

Sample Thesis Statement 5: Math is my worst subject because it bores me, I do not understand it, and I always get too much homework.

The Five-Paragraph Descriptive Essay

How to Write a Five-Paragraph Descriptive Essay

The five-paragraph description essay asks college freshmen to pick one subject and describe it by using words. In other words, students will paint a picture of their subject by the use of language. The subject that students will describe can be a person, place, or thing. This type of essay asks students to use a lot of metaphor and simile, so their description comes alive for the reader. The description for this type of essay should make the reader visualize what the writer's subject looks like. This section will provide a step-by-step recipe/format and a sample to follow when writing the five-paragraph description essay.

I. Recipe/Format for an Introduction:

a). Write two to three general statements about the topic that you will be describing.

b). Show various ways the other people may describe your subject in about two sentences.

c). In one sentence, state your thesis. Your thesis statement should include the subject that you are writing about and three words/phrases that you will use to describe that subject.

Sample of an Introduction:

(a) Everyone who has been to the beach usually loves it. There are various types of beaches. Some beaches are cold in climate and some have warm climate. Moreover, there are some beaches that are rocky and some are sandy. **(b)** Some people would describe the beach as the most beautiful place on earth. There are other people who would describe the beach as the most peaceful place on earth. **(c)** I would describe one particular beach in Maui, Hawaii as sandy, surrounded by crystal clear water, and scenic.

II. Recipe/Format for the 1st Body Paragraph:

a). Start off with two to three sentences that explain your first descriptive word/phrase from your thesis. Tell why that word best describes your subject.

b). Write three to four sentences that give a specific and descriptive example that will paint a picture of your subject by using words.

c). Seal off your paragraph by using one closing sentence.

Sample of the 1st Body Paragraph:

(a) I first would describe one beach in Maui, Hawaii, which is located in Ka'anapali, as sandy. This particular beach has sand that goes for miles and miles. The sand dominates the beach, and there are very few rocks. **(b)** The sand is so smooth on my feet that it feels like I am walking on air. Moreover, the sand is mixed with white, black, and brown grains. These grains are so clear that they actually look like a mixture of salt, sugar and pepper. The sand is so clean, and it looks endless. **(c)** The sand on Ka'anapali beach is breath taking.

III. Recipe/Format for the 2nd Body Paragraph:

a). Start off with a transitional phrase, and write two to three sentences that explain your second descriptive word.

b). Give a three to four sentence descriptive example that illustrates your second descriptive word.

c). Write one closing sentence.

Sample of the 2nd Body Paragraph:

(a) In addition, the beach in Ka'anapali also has crystal clear water. The water is so clear that I can see the sand at the bottom. There are also some areas at the beach where I can see the coral reef. **(b)** The water on this beach is so clear that it looks like a huge plate of glass. The water has no ending or beginning. The water is so clear and calm that it seems as if I could walk on it. The water is clearer than a mirror; it reflects all and makes the sky seem as two. **(c)** I love the crystal clear water on this beach.

IV. Recipe/Format for the 3rd Body Paragraph:

a). Write two to three sentences that explain your third descriptive word. Be sure to start with a transitional phrase.

b). Provide another descriptive example that shows the reader an image of your subject. This example should be set up the same way as your first and second body paragraphs.

(c). Include one closing sentence to seal off the paragraph.

Sample of the 3rd Body Paragraph:

(a) I would finally describe this particular beach as scenic. The scenery on this beach is absolutely breathtaking. It is the kind of scenery that puts you in a meditative state of mind. **(b)** There are palm trees surrounding this beach, which endlessly sway back and forth to the tune of the wind and the sounds of the ocean waves crashing on the sand. There are two neighbor islands, Molokai and Lanai, which seem so close but are far away. There are green mountains, which are surrounding both sides of the beach, and these mountains make me feel that I am enclosed in a different world. **(c)** The scenery on this beach is more than just breathtaking.

V. Recipe/Format for a Conclusion:

a). In about one to two sentences re-state your thesis, but try to re-phrase your thesis statement.

b). Write three to four sentences that will allow you to re-mention all of your specific and descriptive examples from body paragraph one, two, and three.

c). End your essay with one to two closing sentences about your overall topic.

Sample Conclusion:

(a) There are so many ways to describe the Ka'anapali beach in Maui, Hawaii, but the three best ways to describe it are its sandy atmosphere, the crystal blue water, and the breathtaking scenery. **(b)** The sugar, salt, and pepper colored, smooth sand surrounds the beach, and if feels so soft on my feet. The mirror-like water is so clear that I can see the bottom of the ocean and the reflection of the sky. Finally, I love the trees and mountains that overtake the scenery of this perfect beach. **(c)** I gave three descriptive words to describe this beach, but the truth is that I can give a thousand.

The Five-Paragraph Descriptive Essay Supplemental Information

How to Write a Thesis Statement for a Five-Paragraph Description Essay

The five-paragraph descriptive essay asks students to pick a person, place, or thing and write a description. No matter what or whom the student chooses to write about, his/her aim in this type of essay is to paint a picture for the reader by using descriptive words. This type of essay allows students to show off their creativity when it comes to various rhetorical devices, such as metaphors, similes, emphasis of various word or terms, etc.; this type of essay asks students to make comparisons to things, such as the five senses. At the end of the introduction, students will be asked to write a one sentence thesis statement that mentions the person, place, or thing that they are writing about, and that thesis will state three words or short phrases that describe the element being written about. This section will teach students how to write a thesis statement for the five-paragraph description essay; furthermore, this article will provide various sample thesis statements for this kind of an essay.

Instructions for Writing a Descriptive Thesis Statement:

Step 1: Take some time to think about the element that you want to describe.

Step2: If you want to write about a place that you know, then make sure it is a place that you know well. Furthermore, if it is a person whom you choose to write about, then make sure it is a person you know well. Moreover, if it is a thing that you want to write about, then make sure it is something that you know well.

Step 3: After choosing the person, place, or thing that you want to write about, think of three key words or phrases that will allow you to describe your topic. Your descriptive words will be either adjectives or nouns. Furthermore, make sure these words/phrases will allow you to paint a picture with words in your body paragraphs.

Step 4: Write one solid sentence that states what you are writing about, and make sure that you have your three descriptive words/phrases in this sentence. This sentence will be your thesis statement and a body paragraph will be devoted to each descriptive word/phrase.

Step 5: Make sure that your thesis is clear, to the point, and one sentence.

Sample Descriptive Thesis Statements:
Note: No matter what you choose to write about, your thesis statements should look similar to the following samples.

Sample Thesis Statement 1: The island of Maui, Hawaii is the most beautiful place on earth; it has the bluest oceans, the greenest mountains, and the most golden sunsets.

Sample Thesis Statement 2: My best friend Art is great, but he is messy, hyper, and irresponsible.

Sample Thesis Statement 3: The locker room at our college is horrible because it smells really bad, looks like a prison cell, and is very dirty.

Sample Thesis Statement 4: My college campus is outstanding because there are trees all over, the architecture of the buildings is unique, and there is a peaceful Koi pond.

The Five-Paragraph Process Analysis Essay

How to Write a Five-Paragraph Process Analysis Essay

Many college freshmen preparatory English courses will have students write the five-paragraph process analysis essay. This kind of an essay asks students to provide step-by-step instructions on how to do or make something. These instructions should be clear and simple to follow. The process analysis essay works exactly like a "how to" guideline/article; therefore, each student should be highly knowledgeable regarding the topic that he/she chooses to write about. This section will provide a step-by-step guideline and sample of how to write a fully developed and well-organized five-paragraph process analysis essay.

Note: Follow each format and sample paragraph as you would a cooking recipe. Make sure all of the ingredients are in your own paragraphs.

I. Recipe/Format for an Introduction:

a). Start off with about two to three sentences regarding the topic that you will provide instructions for.

b). Write about two sentences that show the reader various ways to approach your subject.

c). Give your thesis statement in one sentence. Your thesis statement should mention the subject that you will be writing about, tell how many steps there are to follow, and list them. Your process analysis may have many steps, but try not to pick something that has over seven, as your essay will be that much longer.

Sample of an Introduction:

(a). Every college course encourages students to edit their own writing. Editing your own work means that you proofread your writing and make sure that it is error free. Moreover, most college classes make students edit their own work, so they can get familiar with turning in clean and presentable writing. **(b)** Some college classes have various ways that they teach editing. Furthermore, some students have their own way of editing. **(c)** There are three basic steps when it comes to editing your own writing; these steps are a content and organization check, a grammar and mechanics check, and one final draft check.

II. Recipe/Format for the 1st Body Paragraph:

a). Write two to three sentences that discuss your first step from your thesis statement. Explain what this step involves.

b). Give a three to four sentence example that illustrates this step.

c). Provide one closing sentence.

Sample of the 1ˢᵗ Body Paragraph:

(a) The first step to take when it comes to editing your writing is a content and organization check. This step requires that you make sure all of your paragraphs are treated with equal length, your entire essay is well organized, and each paragraph has enough information. Moreover, each paragraph should be on topic, which means that there is a topic sentence, explanation and example to support that topic sentence, and a closing sentence. **(b)** For example, I turned in an essay the other day, but when I did my first piece of editing, I realized that one paragraph did not have an example and was shorter than the other paragraphs. When I showed the rough draft to my teacher, he said it would have brought my grade down. I simply added the specific example, which made my paragraph more developed, and it was the same length as my other paragraphs. **(c)** This is the first step to take when it comes to editing your own writings.

III. Recipe/Format for the 2ⁿᵈ Body Paragraph:

a). Start off with a transitional phrase and explain the instructions for your next step. Make sure this explanation is no more than two to three sentences.

b). Provide another illustrative example of your second step. Again, this example should be about three to four sentences long.

c). Seal off your paragraph with one closing sentence.

Sample of the 2ⁿᵈ Body Paragraph:

(a) After fixing your content and organization errors, it is time to proofread for any grammatical and mechanical errors. This process requires that you make sure your essay is free of fragment sentences, run-ons, subject-verb agreement errors, number-agreement errors, tense errors, spelling errors, word choice errors, wordy and/or awkward sentences, comma errors, and other punctuation errors. **(b)** To illustrate, my close friend failed to edit his essay using this second technique in the editing process. His paper received a low grade for grammar and mechanics. Although his paper was perfect regarding content and organization, the teacher marked his paper up because of fragments, run-ons, and spelling errors. **(c)** Proofreading for these types of errors is very important.

IV. Recipe/Format for the 3ʳᵈ Body Paragraph:

(a). Starting with another transitional phrase and in about two to three sentences, be sure to explain the third set of instructions in your process.

(b). Write three to four sentences that give a specific and clear example to portray your third explanation.

(c). End your paragraph with one sentence.

Sample of the 3rd Body Paragraph:

(a) The last step in the editing process is the final draft check. After completing a content/organization and grammar/mechanics check, it is time to make sure that the writing is fully polished. This step requires doing one last run through to make sure that you have caught all errors on all aspects of the editing process. **(b)** For example, there was one essay that I edited for content and organization, and I proofread for grammar and mechanics; however, I did not do one last run through. As a result, I overlooked a few mistakes regarding content/organization and grammar/mechanics. I forgot one closing sentence in one of my paragraphs, and I had two misspelled words. **(c)** One last run through of the essay will ensure that the paper is error free.

V. Recipe/Format for a Conclusion:

(a). In one to two sentences, re-state your thesis, but make sure that you do so using different wording or phrasing.

(b). Briefly re-mention all of your specific examples from your three body paragraphs.

(c). End you essay with one to two closing sentences.

Sample of a Conclusion:

(a) Although many students despise editing, it is important to go through the proper editing process. This process consists of three steps, which are content/organization check, grammar/mechanics check, and a final check. **(b)** When I do not do a content and organization check, I always overlook something, such as the time I forgot a specific example in one of my paragraphs. A grammar and mechanics check is also very important because you could end up with a low grade like my friend who skipped this step in the editing process. Finally, a final check is important to avoid overlooking mistakes, such as forgetting a closing sentence or having a few left over spelling errors. **(c)** The editing process may be long, but it is worth the time in order to have great writing.

The Five-Paragraph Process Analysis Essay Supplemental Information

How to Prewrite a Five-Paragraph Process Analysis Essay

In college, students may be asked to write a process analysis essay for their preparatory English course. The process analysis essay works exactly like a "how to" set of instructions. This type of an essay allows students to explore something that they know really well and teach people how to do it. Students can write an essay on any topic that they know well, such as cooking instructions, home repair, car maintenance, arts and crafts, etc. It is important that students are clear and thorough when writing this type of an essay. Therefore, it is important to take proper time to prewrite. This section will teach students how to prewrite a process analysis essay.

Step 1: Take time to think about a subject that you know well and are an expert in. This type of essay should not contain too many steps or too few steps. It should contain a minimum of three steps and a maximum of five steps. Therefore, students should really take time to think about providing information that does not require heavy duty instructions. It really is best to stick to something basic for this type of an essay, unless your instructor specifies that the assignment is to be lengthy.

Step 2: After choosing the topic that you want to write about, it is a good idea to make a brief list or a free write of how many steps the topic includes and the exact instructions that go along with each step. For the most part, your essay will be five paragraphs long. The body paragraphs will cover the steps. Each step and instructions for those steps will be devoted to a body paragraph. In other words, step one will be devoted to body paragraph one, and steps two and three will be devoted to body paragraphs two and three.

Step 3: When putting together your steps and set of instructions, make sure that each step is specific, clear, and in-depth, but also make sure that it is simplified. In other words, do not make your set of instructions complicated. When writing this type of an essay, it is important to take into account that your reader may never have performed or crafted the topic that you are writing about. After constructing your list or free write and making sure it is thorough and easy to follow, you can go ahead and begin constructing your essay.

How to Write a Thesis Statement for a Five-Paragraph Process Analysis Essay

The five-paragraph process analysis essay asks students to write out instructions or steps to follow for a given topic. In short, the process analysis works just like a "how to" article. The process analysis essay asks students to provide detailed instructions of how to follow a certain element. The writer of this type of essay can provide instructions for a number of topics, such as cooking recipes, fixing household appliances, writing guidelines, etc. The thesis statement for this type of essay will tell your reader the exact number of steps that need to be followed. This section will provide step-by-step instructions on how to write a thesis for a five-paragraph process analysis essay; moreover, this section will provide various sample thesis statements for this kind of an essay.

Instructions for Writing a Thesis Statement for a Five-Paragraph Process Analysis Essay:

Step 1: Although this essay falls under the five-body paragraph category, your instructions may contain more than three steps, so you are free to add one or two more body paragraphs if needed; however, try to limit your instructions to three steps, and be detailed for each of those steps.

Step 2: Take some time to think about a topic that you know well. For example, if you know how to repair a toaster oven, then think about the easiest instructions to provide for your reader.

Step 3: When thinking about the instructions, try to eliminate the amount of steps to follow as much as possible. In other words, if some of your steps coincide, then try to combine them for a solid paragraph and fewer instructions.

Step 4: Now that you have thought about the steps, write a one to two-sentence thesis statement at the end of your introduction that will tell your reader how many steps there will be to follow.

Step 5: After mentioning how many steps there will be to follow, you could also add brief words or phrases of what those steps are; however, unlike other five-paragraph essays, this part is only optional. In other five-paragraph essays, you have to state three things that will tell the reader what your essay will discuss. For this type of essay, there may be more steps involved, so listing everything may be too lengthy. However, if your instructions contain only three to four steps, then you can list them.

Step 6: After writing the thesis, make sure it is short, clear, and to the point.

Sample Thesis Statements for a Five-Body Paragraph Process Analysis Essay:

Note: No matter what topic you want to provide instructions for, your thesis statement should look like the following samples.

Sample Thesis Statement 1: Writing an introduction for a five-paragraph argumentative essay is easy if you follow the three steps; these steps are a generalization of your topic, both sides of your topic, and a thesis statement of your argument.

Sample Thesis Statement 2: Making chicken stir fry contains four solid steps, which are steaming the rice, boiling the chicken, sautéing the vegetables, and then mixing all three things together.

Sample Thesis Statement 3: Rebuilding an engine for a 1965 Mustang contains six solid steps. If you follow the instructions, then you will be able to rebuild an engine for a 1965 Mustang.

How to Write an Introduction for a Five-Paragraph Process Analysis Essay

Most college preparatory English courses will ask students to write a five-paragraph process analysis essay. This type of an essay asks students to explore and provide instructions for something that they know how to do well. In other words, this type of an essay works very much like a "how to" set of instructions or step-by-step instructions. Most students love this type of an essay because it allows them to share their knowledge about various topics. For example, some students can provide instructions about home repair, cooking recipes, auto mechanics, etc. The hardest part for many students is getting started on their essay. This section will teach students how to write an introduction for a five-paragraph process analysis essay.

Step 1: Before students begin their essay, it is important that they consider their topic. Although this type of essay is part of the five-paragraph genre, it can be longer then five paragraphs, as you may have more steps to cover in your essay. The more steps that students have for their process analysis, the more body paragraphs they will need to write. One body paragraph should be devoted to one step.

Step 2: Begin the essay with about two to four general statements about the topic. For example, if you are writing about a cooking recipe, you could discuss what the meal is, where it originated from, or what ethnic background it comes from. The same process would work for any topic that you are writing about. For instance, if you are writing about home repair, you could simply generalize the different methods that people use for home repair.

Step 3: After your general statements about your topic, it is a good idea to provide your reader with a list or description of materials that will be needed for the process. For example, you could simply tell your reader to have such and such items handy. If you are writing about a cooking recipe, then you can list the ingredients that your reader will need. If you are writing about home repair, then you could simply list which tools will be needed. This should be done in about two to three sentences.

Step 4: The final step for the introduction will be the thesis statement. The thesis statement will tell your reader exactly what your essay will be about. For this type of an essay, your thesis statement should be only one sentence, no more than two. The thesis statement will simply tell your reader how many steps your instructions will include; you can also briefly list the steps in short phrases.

The Five-Paragraph Cause and Effect Essay

How to Write a Five-Paragraph Cause and Effect Essay

The cause and effect essay asks college freshmen to examine the cause of one particular subject and discuss the effects of that cause. Most college preparatory English courses teach this type of essay so that students can become more aware of the negative and/or positive effects of the element that they are writing about. Moreover, this type of essay, like all other five-paragraph essays, is designed to teach students how to stay on topic and stay organized with their thoughts. This section will provide a recipe/format and a sample to follow for a fully developed and well-organized five-paragraph cause and effect essay.

Note: Please follow the format as you would follow a cooking recipe. All of the ingredients belong in your own paragraphs. Furthermore, I have provided the lower case letters in the sample paragraphs to illustrate these ingredients.

I. Recipe/Format for an Introduction:

a). Start with two to three general sentences regarding your topic.

b). In about two sentences, discuss the various causes and/or effects of the element that you are writing about.

c). Write your thesis statement. Your thesis should be one sentence, and should mention the one cause of your subject, and the effects of that cause.

Sample of an introduction:

(a) There are many people who like to drink alcoholic beverages. Many people drink for social purposes, and many drink to relax after a hard day of work. Moreover, the notion of alcohol-based drinks has become an influence for many people of all ages around the world, and many abuse it. **(b)** There are some people who believe that there is no cause for drinking. On the other hand, there are people who believe that there are many causes and many effects for drinking beverages that contain alcohol. **(c)** One possible cause of alcohol abuse could be depression for one reason or another; however, the effects of alcohol abuse are liver damage, decrease of brain function, and the loss of a job.

II: Recipe/Format for the 1st Body Paragraph:

a). In two to three sentences, discuss your first effect; explain this first effect.

b). Provide a three to four sentence example that illustrates this effect.

c). Write one closing sentence to seal off your paragraph.

Sample of the 1st Body Paragraph:

(a) One effect of alcohol abuse is liver damage. Alcohol abuse causes cirrhosis of the liver, which shortens the life of a human being. Moreover, liver damage due to alcohol can lead to pain, suffering, and bitterness. (b) For example, my next-door neighbor was an alcoholic; he abused it every day and all day. At the age of forty, he was diagnosed with cirrhosis of the liver. Not only did he experience much pain, but he also spent the rest of his life angry and mad at everything and everyone. (c) If it was not for his alcohol abuse, then he would have lived longer and possibly been happier.

III: Recipe/Format for the 2nd Body Paragraph:

a). Explain your second effect in about two to three sentences, and start with a transitional phrase.

b). Write three to four sentences that provide a specific example of your second effect.

c). Seal off the paragraph with one sentence.

Sample of the 2nd Body Paragraph:

(a) Another effect of alcohol abuse is the decrease of brain function. There have been many studies that show how alcohol kills brain cells, lowers blood flow to the brain, and even causes brain damage. (b) For instance, my uncle was a drinker, and one day my family and I noticed that he was having trouble remembering things. Well, everyday his memory got worse. When we took him to the doctor's office, he was diagnosed with dementia. The doctor told us that dementia could have been prevented if it was not for my uncle's excessive drinking. (c) The effects of alcohol can impact brain function.

IV. Recipe/Format for the 3rd Body Paragraph:

a). Just as you did for body paragraphs one and two, explain your third effect in about two to three sentences.

b). Write another three to four sentence example that portrays your third effect.

c). Give one closing sentence.

Sample of the 3rd Body Paragraph:

(a) Another effect of alcohol abuse could be the loss of a job. When people abuse alcohol, they take on a number of different personality traits, such as laziness or short temper. These personality traits could lead to being fired. (b) To illustrate, my best friend abuses alcohol. Before his alcohol abuse, he had a great job. When he started drinking, he also started showing up to work late, calling in sick, and acting moody with his co-workers and costumers. As a result, he was fired from a great job. **(c)** His alcohol abuse led to his job termination.

V. Recipe/format of a Conclusion:

a). Using different phrasing, re-state your thesis from your introduction.

b). In about three to four sentences, re-emphasize all of your specific examples from your three body paragraphs.

c). Close your entire essay with one to two sentences.

Sample of a Conclusion:

(a) Although there may be many causes for alcohol abuse, there certainly are negative effects. These negative effects of alcohol abuse include liver damage, brain function issues, and losing a great job. **(b)** My neighbor suffered from cirrhosis of the liver due to alcohol abuse; his life was shortened, and he died bitterly. My uncle was diagnosed with dementia due to his alcohol abuse, and the family suffered because of his memory loss. Finally, my best friend lost a perfectly good job due to his alcohol abuse; he became lazy and short tempered. **(c)** The effects of alcohol abuse are certainly not worth it.

The Five-Paragraph Cause and Effect Essay Supplemental Information

How to Prewrite a Five-Paragraph Cause and Effect Essay

Prewriting is one of the most important components of successful college essay writing. In college, students will write many types of essays. Moreover, most preparatory college English courses will teach students the fundamentals of successful essay writing by exposing students to various types of essays and essay writing techniques. One type of essay that students will write in their preparatory college English course is the cause and effect essay. The cause and effect essay asks students to explore at least three effects of a particular cause. Prewriting this type of essay is vital for full organization and development. This section will teach college students how to write a five-paragraph cause and effect essay.

Step 1: The first step is to take proper time to think about your topic. It is never a good idea to simply start writing. Many people do experience writer's block or lack of focus when they simply start writing. Instead, take time to think about one situation and jot down a note or two about that situation. Also, think about several effects that derive from that particular situation. For example, if you think about cigarette smoking, then jot down a few notes of several negative effects caused from cigarettes.

Step 2: Next, take a look at your notes and begin the process of elimination. What that means is that you should try to narrow down your list of effects. Narrow it down to three effects that you feel you can write the most about. Your essay will contain at least five paragraphs, unless directed differently from your professor. This means that each body paragraph will be devoted to a discussion of each effect. In other words, body paragraph one will be devoted to one effect, while body paragraphs two and three will be devoted to the other two effects.

Step 3: The outline process is perhaps one of the most effective finalizations of your prewriting activity. After all of your thoughts are organized and you have the situation and the three effects caused by that situation, begin outlining your introduction, three body paragraphs, and your conclusion.

Step 4: You can arrange your outline to suit you. However, be sure to arrange it in an organized way. Your outline will be a reference for you when you write your final draft of the essay. The outline will keep you organized, so you do not meet any blocks in the final writing process.

Step 5: The outline for your introduction should list your general thoughts about the topic that you will be writing about and your thesis statement. Your thesis statement will discuss the three effects that will be explored in your body paragraphs.

Step 6: Your outline should also map out the body paragraphs. The body paragraphs will list an explanation of each effect, list specific examples, and include other useful developing ideas. The outline should also provide a list that concludes your essay. The conclusion will basically summarize all main points.

How to Write a Thesis Statement for a Five-Paragraph Cause and Effect Essay

The five-paragraph cause and effect essay asks students to examine one object and discuss the effects of that object. For this type of essay, the student should examine the cause of one particular element, and then focus on the after effects of that cause. The cause and effect essay gets students to think more deeply about a particular issue. In fact, the cause and effect essay makes students and the readers of their papers more alert and cautious about the effects of a particular issue. At the end of the introduction, the student will be asked to write one thesis statement that tells three effects that arise from one particular cause. The body paragraphs will focus on the effects. This section will focus on how to write a thesis statement for the five-paragraph cause and effect essay. Furthermore, like previous sections, I will provide some sample thesis statements for the cause and effect essay.

Instructions for the Cause and Effect Thesis Statement:

Step 1: Take some time to think about one particular issue. When you come up with one issue that you would like to examine and write about, be sure to think of one thing that causes that issue. For example, you could write: "Alcohol abuse causes acid reflux disease." Notice how this statement discusses acid reflux and the actual cause of it.

Step 2: After writing the cause of a certain situation, be sure to think of three effects that arise from that cause. Make sure your three effects are either three words or three short phrases. For example, you could write: "Alcohol abuse causes acid reflux disease, and the effects of acid reflux are painful heart burn, erosion of the esophagus, and the need for daily medication." Notice how this statement lists the cause and three short phrases that list the three effects of acid reflux.

Step 3: When completing your thesis statement, make sure that your cause is clear, and make sure that your three effects are clear. Also, make sure your thesis statement is only one sentence. You can get away with two, but try to narrow it down to one sentence for an essay this length.

Step 4: Before moving on to your body paragraphs, make sure that your three effects do not overlap. In other words, make sure your three effects are not the same thing. For example, do not write: "The three effects of acid reflux are heart burn, burning in the chest, and pain when burping." Notice how all of these are the same thing. Be sure all effects are different, so that you can explore your topic and inform your readers about your topic.

Sample Cause and Effect Thesis Statements:

Note: No matter what your topic is, your thesis statement for the five-paragraph cause and effect essay should look like the following.

Sample Thesis 1: Alcohol abuse causes acid reflux disease, and the effects of acid reflux are chronic heart bur, erosion of the esophagus, and daily medication.

Sample Thesis Statement 2: Betrayal from a loved one causes anger, which leads to stress, irrational thinking, and resentment, and all three things are bad for your health.

Sample Thesis Statement 3: Too much sun causes many health issues; the effects of too much sun are skin cancer, second-degree burns, and heat stroke.

The three above sample thesis statements all contain a particular cause of something, and these thesis statements also list the three effects of that particular cause. Also, notice how all three statements are one sentence, and each effect differs from the others in each sentence.

How to Write the Body Paragraphs for a Five-Paragraph Cause and Effect Essay

In this section, I discuss the body paragraphs of this type of essay. The body paragraphs for the cause and effect essay are designed to teach students to stay on topic and to learn the technique of supporting their thesis statement; this is true for all body paragraphs for all the different five-paragraph essays. This section will teach students how to write the body paragraphs for the cause and effect essay. Furthermore, this section will provide a sample of the three body paragraphs that follow the thesis statement for the cause and effect essay.

Instructions for Writing the Body Paragraphs for the Cause and Effect Essay:

Step One: Take time to look at your thesis statement; the thesis will state the cause of something, and it will list the three effects of that cause.

Step Two: Your body paragraphs will focus on the three effects of that cause. Body paragraph one will focus on the first effect from your thesis. Body paragraph two will focus on the second effect from your thesis, and body paragraph three will focus on the third effect from your thesis.

Step Three: For all three body paragraphs, write one to two sentences that explain the effects of the cause. Again, the cause and three effects of that cause are stated in your thesis. One paragraph will be devoted to an explanation for each effect.

Step Four: For all three body paragraphs, write three to four sentences that provide a clear and specific example. The examples need to illustrate the effects and the explanations of those effects. Again, one paragraph will be devoted to each effect, which means that one example in each paragraph is required. Your examples should be something about you, something you know, something you have seen or read, etc., and make sure all examples are different in each body paragraph.

Step Five: For all three body paragraphs, write one closing sentence that will seal off your paragraph. Make sure that all three closing sentences sum up your main point of each body paragraph.

Step Six: Make sure all three body paragraphs provide an explanation of your effect, provide a specific example that illustrates the effects, and have a closing sentence that sums up your main point of each body paragraph.

Sample Body Paragraphs for the Five-Body Cause and Effect Paragraph Essay:

Note: No matter what you topic is, your body paragraphs should follow the above instructions, and your body paragraphs should look like the following samples.

Thesis Statement: Cigarettes cause lung cancer, and the effects of being diagnosed with lung cancer are a shortened life, depression, and anger.

Sample Body Paragraph One: First of all, the effect of being diagnosed with lung cancer is a shortened life. If a person did not smoke, then chances are that he or she would not have been diagnosed with lung cancer and could have lived a long life. For example, a close friend of mine smoked for over forty years. One day he coughed up blood. When he went to the doctor, the doctor told my friend that he had lung cancer due to all the cigarettes he smoked, and he only had about a year to live. Well, at age 45 my friend passed away. If he had not smoked so much, then he might have lived past 70 years of age. A shorter life is the effect of lung cancer.

Sample Body Paragraph Two: Furthermore, the effect of being diagnosed with lung cancer due to cigarettes is depression. Depression can prevent a person from moving on with his or her everyday life. For instance, my neighbor's wife became very depressed after she found out that she had lung cancer from years of cigarette smoking. Well, she became so depressed that she no longer left her house. As a result, she lost her job, and many friends stopped coming to see her. Because of cigarette smoke my neighbor got lung cancer, and because of being diagnosed with lung cancer, my neighbor became depressed and lost much of her everyday life.

Sample Body Paragraph Three: Finally, the effect of being diagnosed with lung cancer is anger. The anger can hurt and push away the people around the person with lung cancer. To illustrate, I watched a movie the other day (I do not recall the title). The main character was diagnosed with lung cancer because he smoked cigarettes for over 50 years. This character became so angry with himself that he verbally abused everyone in his life. Everyone in his life became so hurt that they left the main character to himself. No matter the circumstances, the people in his life did not feel they needed to be treated with abuse. If the main character did not smoke, then he would not have been diagnosed with lung cancer, and if it were not for the lung cancer, he would not have become verbally abusive.

Notice how all body paragraphs support the thesis, explain the effects that are stated in that thesis, provide clear and specific examples to support those explanations, and have a closing sentence to seal off the paragraphs.

The Five-Paragraph Argumentative Essay

How to Write a Five-Paragraph Argumentative Essay

Most basic skills and preparatory college English courses in the United States ask students to write a five-body paragraph argumentative essay. The argumentative essay asks students to take a stand in which they are either for or against a controversial issue. For this type of essay, students must take one side only and defend that side by using clear reasons and specific examples for support. This section will provide students with a full-length step-by-step format to follow when it comes to writing this type of essay. This section will also provide students with a sample argumentative essay that follows the format for each paragraph.

Note: For each paragraph, I provide a guideline of all the elements that belong in each paragraph. After the guidelines for each paragraph, I will provide a sample paragraph. It is important to follow each paragraph as you would a cooking recipe. Just follow the simple ingredients.

I. Format/Recipe for an Introduction:

a) Write about three to four sentences that allow you to immediately introduce your topic. These sentences should be general statements that will tell your reader the central focus of your essay.

b) Provide about two sentences that show both two sides of the argument. For example, "some people are for this, and some people are against that."

c) State your thesis in one clear sentence. Your thesis will tell the reader your stand on the issue that you are writing about. The thesis will also tell the reader three specific reasons why you feel the way you do about your topic.

Sample Introduction for an Argumentative Essay:

Note: In this sample introduction, and in all the other sample paragraphs, I provide the lower case letters to clearly illustrate the above format/recipe. Use the letters as a checklist when you are writing your own essay.

(a) Many cultures believe in arranged marriages. Arranged marriages usually exist in the country of these cultures, such as India and Japan. Furthermore, many of these cultures bring this practice of arranged marriages to the United States, and they force their American raised children into marriages with people whom the children do not love. **(b)** There are many people who are against arranged marriages, especially in the United States. On the other hand, there are many people who believe that arrange marriages should exist in America. **(c)** I believe that arrange marriages should not exist in the United States because they take away freedom, cause depression, and prevent true love.

II. Format/Recipe for Body Paragraph 1:

(a) Start your paragraph with three to four sentences that provide an explanation of your first reason in your thesis statement. Your explanation should tell the reader why you believe in this reason, or why this reason makes you feel the way you do about your main topic.

(b) Write a three to four sentence specific example that illustrates your explanation of your first reason. This example can be about you, someone you know, something you read, something you watched, or something you witnessed, but make sure it is only one example.

(c) Seal off your paragraph with one closing sentence.

Sample of Body Paragraph 1:

(a) First, I am against arranged marriages in the United States because it takes away the freedom that America has to offer. Every person in America has the right to choose what he/she wants to do and whom he/she wants to be with. If people are forced into marriages, regardless of their culture, then it goes against everything that America stands for, which is freedom of choice. **(b)** For example, I have a friend who is part of the Indian culture, but he is American raised. Although his parents live in America, they still forced my friend into a marriage against his free will. Well, the freedom that America offers did not apply to his parents, and my friend did not have the chance to experience the freedom that my other friends and myself got to experience. **(c)** As you can see, America is a land of freedom, but arranged marriages take that freedom away, and everyone who lives here should be able to experience that freedom.

III. Format/Recipe for Body Paragraph 2 :

(a) The same way that you set up body paragraph one, this paragraph will explain your second reason from your thesis. Start this paragraph with a transitional word or phrase, and write a three to four sentence explanation.

(b) Write another specific example that is about three to four sentences long, and make sure that this example is different from the example that you used in body paragraph one.

(c) Provide one closing sentence.

Sample of Body Paragraph 2:

(a) Furthermore, I believe that arrange marriages should not exist in America because it could cause depression. When you are with someone who you do not naturally love, you become unhappy. When you are unhappy, you become depressed. Depression prevents you from living a normal mental and physically healthy life. **(b)** To illustrate, my next-door neighbors have an arranged marriage. The wife explained to my mother that she is very depressed because she did not marry someone she loved, and she was never depressed before this marriage. As a result, she never leaves the house, and she always looks frail when we see her. **(c)** Perhaps if my neighbor did marry someone she loved, then she would not be depressed.

IV. Format/Recipe for Body Paragraph 3:

(a) Starting with another transitional word or phrase, you will explain your third reason from your thesis. This explanation will look similar to your first and second body paragraphs.

(b) Write a third example that differs from your first and second body paragraphs, but make sure that this example is similar in length and supports your third explanation.

(c) Write one final sentence that will allow you to seal off the paragraph.

Sample of Body Paragraph 3:

(a) A final reason why I am against arranged marriages in America is because true love is prevented. When true love is prevented, it becomes challenging to find or be with your soul mate. When a person does not have a soul mate, he/she tends to feel alone and incomplete. **(b)** For instance, I watched a movie a long time ago, which was about a family who immigrated to America with another family. These two families arranged it that their kids would be married when they grew up. When the kids got married, they were not truly in love; they both loved other people. They lost their true soul mates, and they spent their entire marriage feeling alone, lost, and incomplete. **(c)** Life is more fulfilling when you marry the one you love.

V. Format/Recipe for a Conclusion:

(a) In about two sentences, re-state your thesis statement, which is letter "c" from your introduction. However, make sure that you rephrase your wording.

(b) Sum up all of your specific examples from all three-body paragraphs in about three to four sentences.

(c) Provide your reader with one to two intelligent thoughts regarding your overall topic and argument.

Sample Conclusion:

(a) In conclusion, there may be specific reasons why arranged marriages exist; however, I am fully against them existing in America. Arranged marriages prevent freedom of choice, cause depression, and they prevent you from finding your true soul mate. **(b)** My close friend never got a chance to experience the freedom that America offers because his parents forced him into an arranged marriage. Furthermore, my family and I always feel bad for my neighbor's wife, who suffers from deep depression because of her arranged marriage. Finally, if the two characters in the movie that I saw would not have had an arranged marriage, then they would have been able to marry their soul mates and feel more fulfilled and complete in life. **(c)** America offers many choices, and one of those choices should include being with the person you want to spend the rest of your life with. Arranged marriages should not exist in America.

The Five-Body Paragraph Argumentative Essay Supplemental Information

How to Prewrite a Five-Paragraph Argumentative Essay

Most students taking a college preparatory English course will have to write a five-argumentative essay. In this section, I will focus on instructions for prewriting the essay. When students take the time to prewrite, they have a higher chance of turning in a more successful essay; prewriting gives students the chance to organize and develop their thoughts before writing the actual essay. When students take the time to prewrite, they have a higher chance of turning in a more successful essay. This section will teach students how to prewrite an argumentative essay.

Step 1: Take time to think about the topic. For this type of essay, students will have to take a stand either for or against a particular issue. The issue will usually be controversial. Many students face a hard time choosing a side; however, this type of essay requires that students choose a solid side. Students cannot be in between.

Step 2: If you are having trouble deciding whether you are for or against a particular topic, then it is a good idea to make a list or a cluster of the pros and cons. Try to decide which list is bigger. For example, if you have more cons about the topic, then it means that you should probably write an essay that says you are against the issue.

Step 3: After choosing a side, you will have to pick three reasons for your argument. These reasons need to be keywords or phrases. Take time to think about your reasons and think about why these reasons support your argument. Try to do a free write that explores these three reasons. Just simply jot your thoughts down on paper to help develop your thoughts.

Step 4: This final step for prewriting an argumentative essay is the outline. The outline should consist of five Roman numerals **(Refer to the formats/recipes for the entire essay).** Each paragraph will be devoted to a Roman numeral. For example, Roman numeral one will be devoted to the introduction.

Step 5: The outline should also consist of three lower case letters in each Roman numeral, as I show in the format for writing the entire essay. The lower case letters will allow you to write one or two sentences of your main thoughts and supporting details. For example, in the lower case "a" of your introduction, try to mention a general overview of your topic. Lower case "b" will provide both sides and views of the argument. Lower case "c" will state your thesis statement, which will be one sentence that consists of your argument and three reasons why.

Step 6: Roman numerals two, three, and four will be devoted to your body paragraphs. Be sure to outline your thoughts. In each Roman numeral, it is a good idea to provide the three lower case letters, which will consist of three key ingredients. These ingredients are your explanation of your reasons, a clear and specific example, and closing thoughts. Finally, Roman numeral five will be your conclusion, which basically summarizes your essay outline and prewrite.

How to Write a Thesis Statement for a Five-Paragraph Argumentative Essay

The argumentative five-paragraph essay asks students to take a stand on a particular issue. The student's aim in this kind of writing is to persuade his or her reader to see what the writer sees. The introduction of your essay discusses the topic of your essay, and it includes the thesis statement. The thesis statement tells your reader three exact reasons why you are for or against a particular issue, and these reasons will then be discussed in your body paragraphs. This section provides instructions and tips on how to write a thesis statement for an argumentative five-body paragraph essay. Furthermore, this section will provide various examples of thesis statements.

Instructions for Writing a Thesis Statement:

Step 1: When choosing a stand, it is important to know that you have to pick one side, especially for the academic five-paragraph essay.

Step 2: For the most part, your thesis will be one sentence, and it will state three specific reasons for your stand. Be sure to take some time to think about your three reasons.

Step 3: The three reasons in your thesis will be only three words or three short phrases. These three words or short phrases will be exactly what your body paragraphs are about, so make sure they are specific enough to defend your argument.

Step 4: Make sure that your three reasons do not overlap. For example, do not write, "I am against abortion because it is murder, stealing a life, and taking away a life." All three reasons are the same and will not allow you to be convincing in your argument and body paragraphs

Step 5: Make sure your three reasons are all different. For example, you could write, "I am against abortion because it is murder, it could prevent future fertility, and it causes depression." Notice how these three reasons differ from the above example in number 4. These three reasons will allow you to devote a paragraph to each reason, which makes your argument that much more convincing.

Step 6: Check your thesis statement to see if you have all three reasons, and make sure your reasons are clear.

Examples of Various Thesis Statements:

Note: There are a number of topics to argue; usually your instructor will provide a list of topics to choose from. Either way, here are some possible thesis statements that are based on various topics. However, if your topic is different form the examples, then that is okay; just know that no matter what your topic is, you will construct a thesis statement the same way as the examples show.

Abortion:

Thesis 1: I am against abortion because it is murder, it could prevent future fertility, and it causes depression.

Thesis 2: I am for abortion because a person may be facing poverty, the mother could die giving birth, or the child may be born with a severe defect.

Marijuana:

Thesis 1: I am against legalizing marijuana because it causes people to act unsafe, causes minor hallucinations, and causes lung cancer.

Thesis 2: I am for the legalization of marijuana because it eases pain for those who suffer; it opens up appetites for the ill, and it helps people relax.

Pit Bull Dogs:

Thesis 1: I am against the banning of Pit Bulls because they are just like other dogs, they are aggressive only when abused, and the owners are responsible for them.

Thesis 2: I believe that Pit Bulls should be banned because they attack people, they attack other animals, and they are excessively hyper.

The above are only examples of various thesis statements for the five-paragraph argumentative essay. Do notice how all the thesis statements are only one sentence and provide three reasons for each stand. Moreover, all three reasons are different from each other.

How to Write an Introduction for a Five-Body Paragraph Argumentative Essay

The argumentative essay teaches students how to take a stand, defend that stand, persuade the readers to see that stand, and stay on topic with that stand. The five-paragraph argumentative essay is made up of three important components. Those components are an introduction, three-body paragraphs, and a conclusion. For this section, I provide step-by-step instructions that teach students how to write the introduction for a five-paragraph argumentative essay. I will also provide two examples of introductions for this type of an essay.

Instructions for Writing an Introduction:

Step 1: Take some time to think about the topic that you want to write about. After thinking about the topic and deciding on the topic, take some time to think about which side you support. What that means is that you are either for or against something. Remember, this type of essay asks students to pick only one side.

Step 2: After deciding whether you are for or against something, be sure to think of three reasons that tell the reader why you choose the side that you choose.

Step 3: Start your introduction with two to three sentences that provide the reader with a general overview of the topic that you are writing about. This part is not your argument; it is only a few general statements that contain the title of your topic, so that the reader knows what you will be discussing.

Step 4: After writing the general statements of your topic, write about two sentences that provide your reader with two to three sides of the issue. For example, you could tell your reader that some people are for this issue, and other people are against this issue. Remember, an argument always has more than one side; you just have to pick your side.

Step 5: Write a one-sentence thesis statement that states your side. Your thesis will have three reasons that explain your side and tell the reader why you feel the way you do.

Step 6: Make sure your introduction starts with a few general statements about your topic, states different sides to the issue, and has a thesis statement with your stand on the issue.

Sample Introduction for an Argumentative Essay:

Note: No matter what topic you write about, your introduction should look like the following sample.

Sample Introduction 1: Over the years the idea of abortion has been very controversial. There have been many debates regarding abortion when it comes to religious issues and legal issues. Yet, people still have abortions whether it is legal or illegal. Some people believe that abortion should be legal because of freedom of choice. On the other hand, there are many people who believe that abortion should be illegal because they believe that it is murder. Having said that, I believe abortion should be kept legal because the mother may face a life threat during birth, the baby could be born with a defect that will cause suffering to the infant and the family, and the baby could be a product of incest.

Sample Introduction 2: There are many people who smoke marijuana. Marijuana has been around human beings since the beginning of time. Currently, there is a major debate regarding marijuana. The debate deals with legalizing marijuana in California. There are many people who support the legalization of marijuana because they believe that it helps many people with terminal illnesses. One the other hand, there are many people who are strictly against the legalization of marijuana because it causes too many social problems. I believe that marijuana should become legal because it would lower illegal drug trafficking, it is less dangerous than alcohol, and it opens up the appetite for people who are every ill.

Notice how both introductions open up with a few general statements of the topic, show both sides to the issue, and have one clear thesis statement that tells the writer's side and three reasons for the writer's point of view.

How to Write the Body Paragraphs for the Five-Paragraph Argumentative Essay

This section teaches students how to write the body paragraphs for the argumentative essay. This section will teach students how to make sure their body paragraphs support their thesis statements. I will also provide sample body paragraphs that follow the thesis statement.

Instructions for Writing the Body Paragraphs:

Step One: Take time to refer back to your thesis statement, and look at the three words or phrases that you wrote for your argument.

Step Two: Each body paragraph should separately explain your reasons from your thesis, provide a specific example to support those reasons, and have a closing sentence. All your body paragraphs will look like this. For example, body one will talk about the first reason from your thesis, body two will discuss the second reason, from your thesis, and body three will discuss the third reason from your thesis.

Step Three: For body paragraphs one, two, and three, write one to three sentences that explain your three reasons from your thesis. Also, make sure that each paragraph mentions the key words/phrases from your thesis. Your explanations will tell the reader why these reasons make you feel the way you do about the topic that you are writing about.

Step Four: For body paragraphs one, two, and three, write three to four sentences that will provide your reader with a clear and specific example that supports your explanations. These examples should be about yourself, someone you know, something you witnessed, something you read, or something you saw on T.V. Furthermore, each example should differ from the others. For example, in body one if you wrote about yourself, then in body two you can write about something you read or saw on T.V.

Step Five: Make sure that you end all three body paragraphs with one closing sentence. These closing sentences should allow you to seal off your paragraphs.

Step Six: Make sure that all three body paragraphs are fully developed, which means to make sure that all three paragraphs explain your reasons, have an example to support those explanations, and have a closing sentence.

Samples of Body Paragraphs for an Argumentative Essay:

Note: No matter what you topic is, your body paragraphs should look similar to the following samples. Furthermore, the three sample body paragraphs are based on the thesis statement that I provide.

Thesis Statement: I am against the legalization of marijuana because it causes laziness, paranoia, and unsafe activity.

Body 1: First, I am against the legalization of marijuana because it makes people lazy, and if people are lazy, they will not go to school or show up for work. Furthermore, if people are not going to school or work, then unemployment will rise, which creates less contribution to society. For example, I have a friend who smokes marijuana every day. He is always lazy and has even failed to show up to work, so he got fired. Now, he collects unemployment and contributes nothing to society, when there are people who need help at his former job. As you can see, marijuana causes laziness.

Body 2: Secondly, I believe that marijuana causes paranoia, which can lead to a huge mistake with the law. For instance, I read an article about a man who smoked marijuana. Within a few minutes, he felt that his heart was racing and he panicked because he thought that he would have a heart attack. Therefore, he ran down the street yelling and crying, and the police were called, and he was arrested for public disturbance and intoxication. As a result, he now has a police record that will follow him for a long time. Because of the results of paranoia from marijuana, I believe that it should not be legalized.

Body 3: I finally believe that marijuana should not be legalized because it causes unsafe behavior, which could lead to fatal car accidents. Simply, when a person is stoned, he/she is not in the right state of mind, which could cause a person to make an irresponsible decision, such as deciding to drive. I will never forget the day that I was watching the news, and a report of a fatal car accident was announced. The reporters announced that a man driving hit a little kid; the man driving was under the influence of marijuana. Since too many people make bad decisions with alcohol being legal, just imagine what would happen marijuana is legalized.

Notice how all three body paragraphs discuss the three reasons from the thesis, explain those reasons, provide examples for those reasons, and have a closing sentence for each paragraph.

How to Conclude an Argumentative Essay

The argumentative essay asks students to take a stand either for or against a particular issue. For the most part, the issue that students will be arguing will be a controversial issue. Most college English courses will ask their students to write a five paragraph argumentative essay. This section will teach students how to write the conclusion for an argumentative essay.

Step 1: In short, your conclusion should be between five to eight sentences long. The conclusion is simply an emphasis of your entire essay; it summarizes all of your main points. The conclusion should never leave anything open, and it should not offer any new information or ideas if it is not includes in your essay introduction and body. The conclusion is a re-cap of all your major points.

Step 2: Begin your introduction by restating your thesis statement. For this type of an essay, your thesis statement is the last sentence of your introduction. The thesis statement is your argument and the three reasons for your stand. When you re-mention your thesis statement in your conclusion, try to rephrase it, so you are not redundant in your wording. Try to rephrase your thesis statement in about two sentences for complete clarification on your point of view or stand.

Step 3: After restating your thesis statement, be sure that you re-mention all of your main points for your argument. The main points will come from your three body paragraphs. This is the part where you summarize your explanations for all three reasons of your stand, which are the three reasons in your thesis statement. You should also briefly summarize your specific and supportive examples from your three body paragraphs. This should all be done in about four to five sentences, give or take.

Step 4: End your conclusion with one or two intelligent thoughts about your overall essay. These thoughts or statements should be about your overall argument and your point of view. Be sure that these thoughts do not leave anything open or contradict your argument. These thoughts need to be persuasive and stay true to your argument.

Timed In-Class Five-Paragraph Argumentative Essay

How to Write an Timed In-Class Argumentative Essay

In college, most preparatory English classes require students to write one timed argumentative/persuasive essay in order to pass the class and move on to a transfer level English course. This type of essay usually requires the writer/student to read a controversial article or short story. After reading that article/short story, the student is required to pick a side/take a stand for or against that article/short story and then write a five-paragraph essay. The time limit for this type of essay is usually 70-90 minutes. For many students, this task seems harsh, impossible, tormenting, and challenging. However, I assure my reader that following, studying, and memorizing the format/recipe for this type of exam will limit the amount of anxiety for those who have to face this type of writing.

Your timed writing will consist of several elements. These elements include a 70-90 minute time frame, the controversial article/short story that you will read, the instructor's prompt/instructions, and forming your stand/your side of the argument. Having said that, I highly recommend that you read the article/short story and essay prompts twice; it should take about 15-20 minutes. After reading, take about five minutes to decide which side of the issue you are on and be sure to pick only one side. Remember your aim in this is to pick an argument and defend that argument. After deciding which side you are on, think of three reasons why you are for or against the issue. Your three reasons will form your essay.

I. A Format/Recipe of a Timed Introduction:

a) Write about three to four sentences that summarize the main argument or main idea of the controversial article/short story. This portion of your introduction should include the title of the article/short story, the author's full name, and the author's main idea(s).

b) Write about two sentences that provide both sides of the issue (e.g. some people are for this, and some people are against this).

c) Write one sentence that states your thesis. Your thesis will be the one sentence that states your side of the argument and will have three key words or phrases that tell why you are for or against the issue.

A Sample of a Timed Introduction: The lower case letters are a guideline to show how each ingredient from the above format pieces together to form the developed paragraphs. Use these lower case letters as a checklist between all paragraph formats and all of the sample paragraphs.

(a) In the article "America the Promised Land," Oskar, argues that although America is the land of opportunity, it can cause a person to lose his/her identity. Furthermore, Oskar suggests that the melting pot is a "sizzling cauldron" for immigrants who face a loss of cultural identity. Oskar states, "When we come to America seeking to fulfill a dream, we come fragile, vulnerable, and needy. We lose our identity because the influence of American civilization exerts powerful pressure over our former and personal cultural principles." **(b)** There are many people who would agree with Oskar's article because they have either witnessed or experienced such a loss of identity. On the other hand, there are people who completely disagree with Oskar. **(c)** I agree with Oskar, and I believe that people do lose their cultural identity in America because people become materialistic, people experience pure pressure, and people experience racism.

II. A Format/Recipe of a Timed Body Paragraph 1:

a) Write about two to three sentences that explain your first key word/phrase from your thesis. Your explanation should tell why this key word/phrase makes believe what you believe regarding the issue.

b) Write three to four sentences that provide a clear and specific example. Your example needs to 100% support your explanation of your first key word/phrase.

Note: your example should be personal, something you know, something you have seen, watched, read, or from the article that you have to read.

c) Write one closing sentence that allows you to seal off your paragraph.

A Sample of a Timed Body Paragraph 1:

(a) I first believe that many people can lose their cultural identity in America because they become materialistic. Many people in America have the latest technology, such as iPods, iPhones, flat screen TV's, cars, stereo systems, expensive clothes, etc. Therefore, many people from different countries invest in these items and get so wrapped up into them, and they forget about some of their traditional materials from their homelands. **(b)** For example, my family is from Mexico, but I was born in America. My mother tries to preserve and instill her cultural roots into my sister and me. However, I always want the latest Apple Co.'s products. I am so wrapped up into this amazing technology that I never took time or take time to learn about my cultural traditions. I now realize that I have no cultural identity. **(c)** Materialism is a reason why many people lose their cultural identity in America.

III. A Format/Recipe of a Timed Body Paragraph 2:

a) Using a transitional phrase, write two to three sentences that explain your second key word from your thesis. Again, be sure that you explain why this key word makes you feel the way you do about the issue.

b) Write three to four sentences that give a clear and specific example that 100% supports your second explanation.

Note: your example should be a different topic than what you used in your 1st body paragraph. In short, if you already used an example about a movie you saw, then give an example of something else in this paragraph, such as someone you know or something you read.

c) Write one closing sentence to seal off your paragraph.

A Sample of a Timed Body Paragraph 2:

(a) Another reason why I believe that many people lose their cultural identity in America is because they experience peer pressure. Peer pressure among teenagers is very common. Many teenagers feel ashamed that their parents and grandparents are immigrants and still wear traditional clothes and speak their native tongue. Many teenagers feel ashamed because many native-born Americans make fun of these teens and their families; therefore, these teens feel a pressure to assimilate and throw away their language and culture. **(b)** For instance, my best friend's family came from China, and his parents do a great job of preserving their culture; however, when we started middle school, everyone made fun of my friend. After that school year, my friend changed; he stopped speaking his native language at home, and he returned the next school year wearing the latest and most popular clothes; he even changed his name to an American name. My friend's family is sad to see this change in him. **(c)** Peer pressure can change many people; it can especially cause a person to lose their sense of cultural self.

IV. A Format/Recipe of a Timed Body Paragraph 3:

a) Using a transitional phrase, write two to three sentences that explain your third key word from your thesis. Again be sure that you explain why this key word makes you feel the way you do about the issue.

b) Write three to four sentences that give a clear and specific example that 100% supports your third explanation.

Note: your example should be a different topic than what you used in your first body and second body paragraphs. In short, if you already used an example about a movie you saw and someone you know, then give an example of something else in this paragraph.

c) Write one closing sentence to seal off your paragraph.

A Sample of a Timed Body Paragraph 3:

(a) Racism is a third reason why I believe that many people lose their cultural identity in America. Racism causes fear for many people, such as losing a job or getting beat up. This fear can make a person want to identify with another ethnicity and race. **(b)** I read a novel called *The Human Stain*. The story is about an African American who has a light skinned complexion. As a young man, he got sick and tired of being discriminated because of his race; he even lost the love of his life after she found out that he was

African American. Therefore, he feared losing future relationships and job opportunities. As a result, he moved away to another town and identified himself as Caucasian; he threw away his cultural roots and denied his own family. **(c)** Racism is a dangerous thing because it can cause a person to reinvent himself/herself and identify with another ethnicity/race causing a loss of traditions and culture.

V. A Format/Recipe of a Timed Conclusion:

a) Write two sentences that re-mentions the controversial article's title, author, and author's main argument.

b) Write one sentence that re-states your thesis/argument; try to use different word usage. This part is from "c" in your introduction.

c) Write about two sentences that briefly re-mention your all your specific examples from body paragraphs one, two, and three.

d) Write one to two sentences of an intelligent final thought that will seal off your entire essay.

A Sample of a Timed Conclusion:

(a) In Oskar's article, he argues that America is a land of opportunity, but it is also a land that causes people to lose their cultural identity. **(b)** I believe materialism, peer pressure, and racism are three factors that cause a person to lose their cultural identity in America. **(c)** I am so wrapped up into the latest technology that I never take time to carry my family's traditions from Mexico. Due to peer pressure, my best friend changed his Chinese name into an American name, stopped speaking his native language, and started wearing popular American clothes. In the novel *The Human Stain*, the protagonist stopped identifying himself as African American and identified himself as Caucasian all because he could not take the racism that he experienced as a black man. **(d)** America is a beautiful country filled with opportunity, but a person can easily become lost in this country. However, there is nothing or no one to blame for these losses; it is up to each individual to choose what he or she wants to preserve and never let anyone tell him/her what they are or should become.

Always take time to proofread for content/organization and grammar/mechanics. For a timed writing, there will be errors, but try to allow yourself at least 5-10 minutes to do a quick run through to catch excessive errors.

The Five-Paragraph Personal Development/Self-Reflective Essay

How to Write a Five-Paragraph Personal Development/Self Reflective Essay

In college, many students will be asked to write a personal development essay also known as a self-reflective essay. Either a preparatory English course or a guidance course will ask students to write this type of an essay. This kind of an essay can be very rewarding, and it allows students to look deep within themselves for further self-discovery. This type of essay will ask students to write about their flaws/weaknesses and/or good qualities/strengths. This section will provide two sample personal development/self-reflective essays. One sample explores negative traits/weaknesses, and the other explores the positive traits/strengths.

Positive Traits/Strengths:

I. A Format/Recipe for and Introduction:

a) Write two to three general sentences about the great qualities that exist in human nature.

b) Write two sentences that mention different ideas that other people may consider good qualities.

c) Write a one-sentence thesis that tells what your three qualities are.

A Sample of an Introduction: Use the lower case letters in each sample paragraph to see how the above formats piece together to form the paragraphs.

(a) There are many things that count as good qualities. Many people have a lot of good qualities, and there are many people who have few good qualities. The people who know their good qualities and put them in practice can really improve the quality of life for themselves and for others around them. **(b)** Some people may consider those who do volunteer work is a good quality. On the other hand, there are people who believe a person who is disciplined in health and work are good qualities. **(c)** I believe that I have three distinct qualities; they are my ability to be funny, forgiving, and helpful.

II. A Format for Body Paragraph 1:

a) Write two to three sentences that explain your first quality. Tell the reader what you mean by this quality.

b) Write three to four sentences that provide your reader with a clear and specific example that supports your first quality. This example should show your reader your quality, not just tell.

c) Write one closing sentence to seal off your paragraph.

A Sample of Body 1:

(a) My first quality is that I am funny. I have the ability to make people laugh. I make people laugh because of my jokes, and I am really hyper. People laugh at my sarcastic sense of humor and impersonations. **(b)** For example, the other day at work, all of my co-workers were in a sluggish mood. There is one co-worker who nobody likes because of his bad attitude. This particular co-worker was not at work that day, and he has a really funny accent and walk. Well, I started imitating this person, and all of my co-workers started laughing, even our boss was laughing. The day was perfect after that, and everyone was in a good mood. **(c)** I love making people laugh because it also makes me feel good.

III. A Format/Recipe for Body Paragraph 2:

a) Using a transitional phrase, write two to three sentences that explain your second quality.

b) Write three to four sentences of another specific example that shows the reader this quality.

c) Write one closing sentence to end this paragraph.

A Sample of Body Paragraph 2:

(a) Another great quality about me is that I am a very forgiving person. I believe that no matter how damaging a person's actions are, you should always forgive him/her. I think that being forgiving helps me feel more positive and healthier. **(b)** For instance, I have been best friends with my childhood friend for over twenty years. Well, a few years ago, my friend stole $100 from me. I was very upset, but about one year later he apologized and explained why he did it, and I forgave him. We are still best friends. **(c)** Forgiveness is sometimes hard, but when people do forgive, they feel a lot better.

IV. A Format/Recipe for Body Paragraph 3:

a) Using another transitional phrase, write two to three sentences that explain your third quality.

b) Write three to four sentences of another specific example that show the reader this quality.

c) Write one closing sentence to end this paragraph.

Sample of Body Paragraph 3:

(a) The third quality that I have is that I am a person who likes to help others. When I help someone, I feel good knowing that I contributed something to the world. I believe that helping others is everybody's responsibility as a human being. Furthermore, when I help someone, I never expect anything in return. **(b)** To illustrate, the other day I was working very hard on my homework at the college; however, another student came into the lab where I was working. This student had tears in her eyes because she did not understand how to write her essay. Although I did not know who this student was, I set my work aside to help her piece together her essay. I ran into her a day or so later, and she got an A on the assignment. **(c)** Helping other people is something that I consider a great quality about myself.

V. A Format/Recipe for the Conclusion:

a) Write two to three sentences that re-state your thesis (your three qualities).

b) Write two to three sentences that re-mention all your specific examples from body paragraphs one, two, and three.

c) Write one to two closing sentences of any final intelligent thoughts about your qualities.

A Sample of a Conclusion:

(a) Despite any other qualities that I may have or may not have, it is the three qualities of being funny, forgiving, and helping that shape my outlook on life. **(b)** I love making people laugh, just like I did for my co-workers the day that they were all sluggish. I also believe that forgiveness can promote a healthier lifestyle, and that is why I forgave my friend who stole money from me. Finally, I love helping others because it makes me feel positive, such as the time I set my work aside to help that student with her essay. **(c)** Everyone possesses great qualities, and if everyone would put them into practice, then the world would be a better place.

Negative Traits/Weaknesses:

I. A Format/Recipe for and Introduction:

a) Write two to three general sentences about flaws that exist in human nature.

b) Write two sentences that mention different ideas that other people may consider to be flaws.

c) Write a one-sentence thesis that tells what your three flaws are.

A Sample of an Introduction: Use the lower case letters in each sample paragraph to see how the above formats piece together to form the paragraphs.

(a) There are many things that count as bad qualities in every human being. Many people have many flaws, and there are many people who have few flaws. The people who know their bad qualities and work hard to eliminate these flaws can really improve the quality of life for themselves and for others around them. **(b)** Some people may consider those who have bad tempers a flaw. On the other hand, there are people who believe that laziness is a bad quality. **(c)** I believe that I have three distinct flaws; they are being impatient, being conceited, and working too much.

II. A Format for Body Paragraph 1:

a) Write two to three sentences that explains your first flaw. Tell the reader what you mean by this flaw.

b) Write three to four sentences that provide your reader with a clear and specific example that supports your first flaw. This example should show your reader your flaw, not just tell.

c) Write one closing sentence to seal off your paragraph.

A Sample of Body 1:

(a) My first major flaw is that I am impatient. I never like to take the time to wait for things. The bad thing about this flaw is that I make other people around me nervous when they start to see that I am getting impatient. **(b)** For example, the other day I went to a fast food place with my best friend, and there was a really long line with only one cashier. Because I am impatient, I started to sigh, and the people in front of me and behind me started to get agitated. In addition, my friend kept telling me to calm down; I could tell that he was nervous with my complaining. I ended up telling the casher to get more help. **(c)** I know that my impatience is a bad flaw, and I do need to work on that.

III. A Format/Recipe for Body Paragraph 2:

a) Using a transitional phrase, write two to three sentences that explain your second flaw.

b) Write three to four sentences of another specific example that shows the reader this flaw.

c) Write one closing sentence to end this paragraph.

A Sample of Body Paragraph 2:

(a) Another bad flaw that I have is that I am conceited. I am always worried about the way I look, and I always make sure that I look good. In the end, I know that this flaw makes me look bad, and it makes me look like an insensitive person. **(b)** For Instance, I was at school last week, and my friends and I were meeting at the cafeteria before class. One of my friends was talking about a problem he was having, but I was worried about how I looked and if the clothes I was wearing made me look good. I was wandering this because there was a girl who I wanted to go talk with. All my friends said that I was conceited. **(c)** I know that I need to work harder to control this flaw, so that my attention can be on other things that require my attention.

IV. A Format/Recipe for Body Paragraph 3:

a) Using another transitional phrase, write two to three sentences that explain your third flaw.

b) Write three to four sentences of another specific example that shows the reader this flaw.

c) Write one closing sentence to end this paragraph.

A Sample of Body Paragraph 3:

(a) A third flaw that I have is that I am a workaholic. For some reason, I never stop working in school or my job. The really bad thing about this flaw is that I allow my work to take time away from the people in my life, which destroys relationships. **(b)** To illustrate, I had a girlfriend who I loved very much, and she loved me. Unfortunately, I had a hard time controlling the amount of hours that I put into work. She talked to me about the little time I make for her, but I did not change; she deserved better and someone who was not a workaholic. Therefore, she did break up with me, and I do not blame her. **(c)** Being a workaholic is hard for me to control, but I know that I need to work on this flaw so that further relationships are not destroyed.

V. A Format/Recipe for the Conclusion:

a) Write one to two sentences that re-state your thesis (your three flaws); however, do avoid stating the same sentence.

b) Write three to four sentences that re-mention all of your specific examples from body paragraphs one, two, and three

c) Write one to two closing sentences of any final intelligent thoughts about your flaws.

A Sample of a Conclusion:

(a) Despite that fact that I may have many flaws, the three main flaws that I need to work on are my impatience, my conceitedness, and my problem with being a workaholic. **(b)** I know that when I am impatient; it makes other people around me uncomfortable and nervous, such as my friend at the fast food place. I also know that when I am conceited, it makes people, such as my friends, think that I am selfish. Furthermore, the fact that I am a workaholic destroys my relationships. I lost a great girl because of this problem. **(c)** Everyone has flaws, and those flaws are part of who we are, but everyone also has great qualities, and one of those great qualities that exist for all human beings is the fact that we can all change. After writing this, I have a better understanding of my flaws, and I will work hard to eliminate them.

Made in the USA
Coppell, TX
30 June 2020